Saving the Earth

Akuppa

(W) indhorse Publications

Published by
Windhorse Publications Ltd.
38 Newmarket Road
Cambridge
CB5 8DT, UK
email: info@windhorsepublications.com
www.windhorsepublications.com

© Akuppa 2009

First Edition published as *Touching the Earth* 2002
Second edition (revised) 2009

The right of Akuppa to be identified as the author
of this work has been asserted by him in accordance
with the Copyright, Designs and Patents Act 1988

Cover design by Peter Wenman
Cover image © Windhorse Publications Ltd.
Printed by Bell & Bain Ltd., Glasgow

British Library Cataloguing in Publication Data:
A catalogue record for this book is available from the British Library

ISBN: 9781 899579 99 0
ISSN 2041 - 2509

As this work is not of a scholarly nature, Pali and Sanskrit words have been
transliterated without their diacritical marks.

About the Author

Akuppa (John Wigham) was born and bred on Tyneside in Northern England in 1962. Having been interested in nature from a young age, he studied geography and town planning. He went on to work in local government in Manchester, Sunderland and North Tyneside, with a particular involvement in environmental matters. He has campaigned politically on green issues, especially climate change, for many years. He was ordained into the Western Buddhist Order in 2000, and given his Buddhist name 'Akuppa', which means 'unshakeable'. He teaches meditation and Buddhism at Newcastle Buddhist Centre, and in prisons, where he serves as a Buddhist chaplain.

Acknowledgements

Time has not dimmed my gratitude to those who helped in different ways when I was preparing the first edition of this book – Jnanasiddhi, Subhadassi, Ratnaprabha, David Cornwell, Dayajit, Toby Smith, Arthur and Betty Wigham, Pauline and John Pearson, and the entire island of Lindisfarne. I also wish to thank all those at Windhorse Publications, past and present, who have been unstintingly helpful.

It might be obvious from the references in the book that I owe a debt of gratitude to two particular influences. First, for my imperfect understanding of Buddhism, I am indebted, for the understanding but not the imperfection, to my teacher Urgyen Sangharakshita, and, through him, to Padmavajra and the many others in the Western Buddhist Order who have offered an unbounded wealth of insight and friendship. Secondly, for helping me to deepen my understanding of our current predicament, I warmly acknowledge the vivid and vivacious influence of Joanna Macy.

My thanks also go to other teachers, inspirers and fellow travellers in exploring the territory of earth-loving Buddhism, especially Saramati, Parami, Maitrisara, Akasati, Lokabandhu, Guhyapati and Kamalashila. For a good supply of Marmite and many other practical acts of kindness when I was writing this version at the Ecodharma Centre in Catalonia, I thank Guhyapati, Carol, Yashobodhi, Kamalashila and Rob.

Contents

1

The Path Starts
at Your Feet

BY THE TIME I BEGAN TO FOLLOW THE BUDDHIST PATH,
I already had a long-standing personal interest in environmental issues. I had been engaged in them as a planner,
local politician, and campaigner. It was clear to me from the
outset that there was some affinity between Buddhism and
environmental concern. Since then, with the help of others,
I have reflected on what that affinity is and on how these
two areas of my life might fit together. I thought for a time
that Buddhism might need to be changed to accommodate
modern environmental concerns. More and more, however,
I have come to be convinced that the essence of the Buddha's
teachings is timeless. The path of transformation they offer
is of immense value to the environmental movement, and,
indeed, to any human being in the modern world. It also
seems to me that a love for the environment is a natural and
even indispensable part of being a Buddhist.

In this book, I explore the valuable gifts that Buddhism has
to offer environmentalism, as well as the importance to the

Buddhist of an environmental perspective. It is my hope, as a traveller on this path, to set out a rough map of the terrain, as much for my own benefit as anyone else's. I hope that, having surveyed it, you will feel inspired to explore further through the many other resources, books and websites on the subject, some of which I list at the end of the book.

The virtue of a path is that it starts right at your feet. Whatever mix of feelings you have at this moment about the state of the environment, that is where we begin. Buddhism is not about gritting one's teeth and suppressing feelings that we might find difficult. Nor is it just another intellectual, political, or even religious position. It is not to be plundered as a source of bland homilies about compassion or the nature of the universe. Its true value lies in the practical path of transformation that it offers, both for us and for the world. To test this, we will need to engage our hearts as well as our minds.

I have to confess that, when I hear a radio programme or see a magazine article about the destruction of the Amazonian rainforest, my immediate reaction is to want to switch channels or turn the page. It's not that I don't care about the rainforest. It's just that the inevitable statistics about the rate of its disappearance (often measured in pieces of land the size of Wales) are simply too depressing. I already know about the issue, I don't buy tropical hardwoods, and there seems to be little else I can do about it. What could I, as one person, possibly do that would make anything more than the most minute difference? Why just make myself miserable?

Such feelings of despair and powerlessness are common reactions to global environmental problems. The complex of conditions that bring them about seems too vast and too distant to exert any influence over whatsoever. This can result in a kind of alienated fatalism: we carry on with our lives, but with a dull sense of anxiety and pessimism about the future.

We can always choose to listen only to the more reassuring experts or, indeed, not to listen to any at all. Messengers of doomsday are not, after all, a new thing, but, as yet, no all-consuming apocalypse has overtaken us. Those of us without the benefit of several scientific degrees have to rely on the say-so of experts to judge the nature and extent of the environmental crisis. This can be a bewildering experience. Scientists often disagree about the facts, or they agree about the facts but come up with different interpretations of them. Almost weekly we read of new research findings and new predictions, sometimes alarming, sometimes reassuring, but a substantial majority of scientific opinion is pointing out the catastrophic and irreversible consequences of our actions. Even if the thousands of scientists working for respected organizations such as the Intergovernmental Panel on Climate Change and the International Union for Conservation of Nature might be getting it wrong, the stakes are so high that it would be foolish not to take them seriously. If we waited until the evidence was completely incontrovertible, it would be too late to do anything about it anyway. We can deny the evidence, or we can acknowledge that it matters.

The desire to continue with business as usual, to avoid any implications we don't like, can be very strong. If you think you may have exceeded your overdraft limit, you might be tempted not to open your bank statements, believing, somewhere in the back of your mind, that this will make the problem go away. It doesn't work, I have found, yet this is exactly how we as a society behave with regard to some environmental issues.

Another 'difficult' feeling that we may be starting with is anger. The sense of frustration at the slowness of our collective response to climate change, for example, can be overwhelming. It's like watching some terrible, avoidable accident happen in slow motion and not being able to intervene. Despair and anger are not unnatural responses to the situation; they are even understandable. But, somehow, we need to get to the point where we can face up to the problems, work out the implications, and act accordingly. If we are stuck in such negative feelings, we are likely to overlook the very thing that can help us move on. The fact that we have felt despair in the first place indicates that we must have at least some spark of concern about other people, about future generations, about animals, or about the beauty of nature. If we feel anger, that shows that we have a well of energy we can draw upon. It is this capacity to look beyond ourselves that makes a truly human existence possible. This seed of heroism is the most precious part of being human.

The Buddhist path is about being fully human, in the most positive sense. It calls us to be truly happy, even blissful. We may think that we have a choice between personal happiness on the one hand, and being alive to the state of the world on the other. It's true that we need to avoid a gloomy obsession with suffering in the world – that doesn't help anyone. But ultimately, Buddhism says, the way to lead a rich, fulfilling, and, yes, blissful life is to be fully alive to the world around us.

So what would a Buddhist environmentalism be like? What Buddhism and environmentalism share is a desire to end suffering. Perhaps it would be more fruitful then to think not of a Buddhist environmentalism, but Buddhism as environmentalism. It will not be another ideological position, nor a political platform. It will be what it has always been – a path of transformation that involves every part of us – body, heart, and mind. The path is heroic, but it does not lead us to sacrifice our deepest longing for happiness. Along the Buddhist path, feelings of despair and powerlessness are merely the seeds of change. They can be cultivated and grown. If we do look beyond ourselves and follow the path, we might be surprised to find that, in a thousand ordinary ways, real change is possible after all.

2

The Awakening Heart and Mind

IMAGINE YOU ARE SITTING on one of the Pacific islands of Tuvalu. Opposite you is a woman called Tubwebwe.[1] As you talk, she is patiently straining the juice of a noni fruit to produce a remedy for breathing difficulties, a cure that has been handed down the generations. She enjoys life on the island, surrounded by family and friends in a traditional society that makes its living from the sea. As she looks over to her three children playing nearby, her smiling face is clouded by an expression of anxiety. She has been told that the sea is rising and that within a generation or two, the islands may disappear. What will become of her home, her children, her friends' children? What will become of their way of life?

Imagine you are in a crowded slum area of Dhaka, Bangladesh, talking with a twenty-year-old woman called Honufa.[2] She talks about the conditions in which she lives: 'Every day there is disease in this slum; diarrhoea, dysentery, stomach pains, and headaches. Children suffer the most.

Everything is packed into a tiny space here, you can imagine the unhealthy situation we live in. I've lost a two-year-old son from a diarrhoeal disease and there are two other women in this room that I know have also lost children to diarrhoea due to the unsanitary conditions here.'

Imagine you are in what remains of the cloud forests of the Virunga Volcanoes in eastern Africa. Much of the forest has already been lost to logging and encroachment for agriculture. Through the moss-covered trees, you hear the grunting and barking of a group of about ten mountain gorillas. They are keeping track of each other as they move through the forest eating shoots and leaves. You catch a glimpse of some of them, strong and powerful, yet gentle and shy. Due to logging, disease, and poaching, only about seven hundred of them survive.

We are living in a world of extremes. A small minority of the world's population lives in unprecedented affluence, reaping the fruits of new technology and the increasingly global economy. For a much greater number of people, existence is marginal. In one way or another, they are struggling to cope with rapid changes that are happening all over the world. Cities across Asia, Africa, and Latin America are expanding so rapidly that millions of children are left to fend for themselves on the streets. Pacific islanders face the prospect of losing their homes as sea levels rise. Wild places and their animals and plants are being lost to exploitation and urbanization.

How are we to respond, looking upon this world from the vantage point of a comfortable, affluent society?

Our predicament is not entirely new. Siddhartha Gautama, who would become known as the Buddha, was born about 2,500 years ago to a privileged élite in the emerging urban civilization of the Ganges Basin. His parents were wealthy and powerful and he was brought up with all the wealth, security, and status that his society could offer. He enjoyed a happy childhood inside his parents' palace. But when he grew to be a young man, he became dissatisfied with his lifestyle, feeling hemmed in by assumptions and expectations. One day, while riding through the streets of his home city in his chariot, he was struck by the reality of human suffering. He saw sickness, old age, and death as though for the first time, and realized that no one, rich or poor, could escape them.

How do we respond to suffering?

The world that we look upon in our day is vastly more complex than the one in which Siddhartha lived. In his time, technology was relatively simple, the scale of human activity relatively small, and the relationship between people and the land still relatively local. Nowadays, not only are there many more people, but the technological energy at our disposal is far greater. Networks of actions and their consequences spread out across the whole world.

It often feels as though we are bombarded with images of suffering. Not only this, but the causes of suffering also seem bewildering in their complexity. This can make our temptation to screen ourselves from it all the greater.

There are all sorts of ways in which we can do this. Outright denial is just one of them. Perhaps we are reluctant to face up to the implications for our own lives. Sometimes people simply cannot take in the enormity of the problem, and understandably so. Even some Jewish people in Europe at the time of the Holocaust refused to believe what was going on around them – it was just too big to comprehend. Nowadays there are still many who flatly deny the possibility of human-induced climate change. I'm not talking here about those who honestly wish to question the evidence (we should all do that), but rather those who seem to come to the subject with minds made up, because of vested interests or because they simply don't want to believe it.

Even if we are forced by the sheer weight of evidence to acknowledge that there might be a problem, it does not mean that we will necessarily take the appropriate action. For many of us, the evidence for climate change still comes through media reports about scientific findings, along with, perhaps, the odd bit of unseasonal weather. It is still possible – for the time being – to carry on a high-consumption, high-pollution lifestyle. Everyone else, it seems, is still doing it.

A friend of mine was in a department store when the fire alarm sounded. Some people started walking calmly towards the exits, others looked to the staff for guidance but found that they were just as uncertain what to do. Many, however, no doubt assuming it was a false alarm, blithely carried on with their shopping. This is the way we all too often behave; rather than take responsibility for our actions, we look to those in authority, or we just go along with what everyone else does. Unless we can see and smell the danger for ourselves, we will tend to carry on as usual. In the world at the moment, the alarm bells are ringing, but the most serious danger is not so much to us, but to future generations and to people in other parts of the world. If we look to those in government, we see indecision or complacency. If we look to those around us, we see many people carrying on as usual.

This is similar to what some psychologists call the by-stander effect. If, say, someone collapses on a busy street, it might be that nobody comes to help. Everyone is waiting for someone else to take the initiative. Perhaps they are afraid to get involved, or even afraid to stand out from the crowd.

Another kind of response would be the kind of paralysed despair that I referred to in the opening chapter. You acknowledge the problem, but it seems too big or too distant for you to do anything about it. This locks us into a particularly unhappy state, a life of powerless depression.

In recent years, as the evidence has mounted up, it has become more and more difficult for people to deny the scale of environmental problems in the world. This may be giving way, though, to another response – survivalism. Here, we acknowledge the scale of the problem, but rather than try to bring about change, we narrow our field of concern to ourselves and perhaps those near to us. We focus on survival strategies for ourselves or our families. This thinking can also affect global thinking. There is a tendency in many developed parts of the world to want to insulate themselves from global instability and to pull up the drawbridges of 'Fortress North America', 'Fortress Europe', or 'Fortress Australia'.

So there is a whole range of ways in which human beings respond to collective threat – you may be able to think of others. Perhaps you have experienced particular situations or emergencies where you have seen these reactions – denying, ignoring, despairing, or not caring – being played out. And as human beings, we are fallible. It would be a rare person who has not fallen prey to one or more of these at some time in their lives.

So these critical situations throw into sharp focus the very fundamental question – what sort of person do we want to be, what sort of life do we want to lead? Do we want to be the kind of person who shies away from taking action, or who just looks after themselves? Or do we want to become the kind of person who has the presence and courage to help others? As an example, let us return to the story of Siddhartha.

Going forth

Siddhartha could have put his experience of suffering from
his mind and settled back into a comfortable life of privilege.
No doubt there were many voices urging him to do so. In the
end, though, they did not prevail and Siddhartha decisively
left behind all the wealth and security of his position. He
embarked on a quest to end suffering – not just the actual
suffering he had witnessed while riding around his home city,
but all suffering. He wanted to get to the root of suffering,
through sickness, old age, and death. He wanted to get to the
root of his own feelings of being hemmed in, struggling to
find a sense of purpose and fulfilment.

We can imagine that the Buddha would have needed some
determination and courage to leave behind everything that
was familiar to him, everything that gave him security. He
must have been very clear in his mind about the unsatisfac-
toriness of palace life, for himself and those he loved. But
he must also have had a positive sense of a better way, a call
to adventure, a sense of opening to the possibilities of life.
Stealing through the night on his horse, he had let go of all
the conventional expectations placed on him, all the narrow
ways he was being defined. No doubt there will have been fear,
but there must also have been a real sense of surrendering to
life, a great upwelling of freedom and energy.

Soon after setting out on his quest, Siddhartha swapped
his expensive clothes for rags and cut his hair. Both would
have been a mark of his status. He then went to live in the
forest with those who seemed to share his purpose most
closely – the holy men, common in India at the time, who had
dedicated themselves to meditation and ascetic practices as a
way to the truth.

Siddhartha was nothing if not wholehearted. We could try to emulate him quite literally, climate permitting, by taking to the wilderness ourselves. But there are other ways of following in his footsteps. They might not entail wearing rough clothes or leaving home, but they will mean putting wealth and status aside to some extent and embarking on a quest of our own to find the nature and cause of the world's problems.

What is the problem?

A search for the causes of the global environmental crisis will take us through the realms of ecology, biology, climatology, politics, economics, sociology, and many other areas of knowledge. One could no doubt spend a lifetime reading up on the subject before getting around to doing anything to help. Let's begin by taking an objective overview of what the main environmental problems are.

Climate Change. The vast majority of scientific experts believe that human-induced climate change is already occurring and that further change is inevitable. It is not a question of whether the earth's climate will change, but rather by how much, where, and how soon. Large parts of southern Africa, the Middle East, southern Europe, and Australia are becoming more arid. In tropical and subtropical countries, agricultural production is decreasing and diseases such as malaria and dengue are on the rise. Tens of millions of people (perhaps many more) are likely to be displaced by rising sea levels. Delicate ecological systems such as coral reefs, mangroves, and tropical forests are endangered. Many believe the effects are already with us and that recent sea level rise, increasing frequency of floods, droughts, heat waves, and heavy rain in recent years are human-induced.[3] Some scenarios are more serious still. The

18

collapse of the Western Antarctic Ice Sheet into the sea could, for example, lead to a global sea level rise of ten metres, which would inundate major cities such as London.

Pollution. It is not just the headline-hitting incidents such as oil spills and nuclear power plant disasters that do the harm. Day by day, the poisoning of the air, land, rivers, and sea continues unpublicized. For example, each of us, on average, throws away seven times our own bodyweight in rubbish each year.[4] If you add the amount of waste from manufacturing and delivery, the figure is much higher. Household rubbish is laced with toxic substances – chemicals, heavy metals from cleaning fluids, batteries, computers, PVC, and so on. Whether it is dumped in holes or burned, it lingers as a threat to human and animal health and has been blamed for increasing rates of cancer, birth defects, asthma, and allergies. In the oceans, birds and mammals are being killed by the vast amounts of plastic we've discarded – balls, toothbrushes, shopping bags. One estimate says that there are 46,000 such pieces of flotsam in every square mile of ocean.[5]

Species Extinction. It is undisputed that species are disappearing rapidly as their habitats are put under pressure from agriculture, pollution, urbanization, roads, and climate change. Biologists estimate the current rate of extinction to be between a hundred and a thousand times greater than it was before humans appeared.[6] It also seems to be increasing. The biologist E.O. Wilson has estimated that, at current rates, half of all species will be extinct in 100 years.[7] Elephants, tigers, pandas, polar bears, hippopotamuses, mountain gorillas, and whales are already endangered, but the list includes many less enchanting varieties of plant, worm, beetle, and fungus. Many of these are vital to the forms of traditional medicine on which most people in the world depend.[8] While there have been isolated successes in rescuing species from extinction, in most cases conservation efforts have proved too little, too late.[9] The current mass extinction differs from those in the past because it is not only species that are being wiped out, but habitats. The pace of change is so fast that wildlife cannot migrate or adapt quickly enough to keep up.

Effects on people. As the world's population grows, pressure for food production and water supply increases. Over the past fifty years, to satisfy our desire for food, water, timber, fibre, and fuel, we have changed nature more rapidly than at any other time in human history. This is leading to irreversible changes. While some parts of the world have the technological and economic capability to adapt, in other places this could lead to the sudden, unexpected collapse of ecosystems. Loss of water supplies, food shortages, collapse of fisheries, the eutrophication (the reduction of oxygen caused by an excess of nutrients and growth of algi) of coastal waters, floods, and disease could all become more frequent. The brunt of the effects are likely to be felt by regions such as sub-Saharan Africa which are already the poorest. Rural people who are more directly reliant on their environment for their liveliloods are the most vulnerable to change. Many could become refugees, leading to increased political tension and widespread violent conflict within developing countries. This could also affect the wealthier parts of the world.[10]

Searching for the causes

The debates about environmental causes and effects will no doubt run and run. But how much evidence do we need before we decide that it's time to act? Whatever we conclude about the details, there is enough evidence to suggest that, at least as a matter of sensible precaution, radical changes are needed in our relationship to the environment. To gamble that our best climate scientists are deluded is, as the writer Colin Butler has observed, akin to Russian roulette. 'The inertias involved mean that we cannot wait for certainty. Certainty does not mean safety.'[11] We need to look not just at the symptoms but also at the underlying causes.

One way of looking at the problem is in terms of our relationship to technology. The environmental problems we face have been brought about by the systematic overuse of increasingly powerful technologies. The internal combustion engine and agricultural mechanization came about to help people travel more easily and to grow more food. But what may be beneficial to the individual begins to have harmful consequences for everyone when replicated by millions. New inventions set up whole new patterns of resource use and pollution, and enable social and political changes that are practically impossible to reverse. People have not necessarily set out to do harm, but they have not been able to foresee, or have chosen to ignore, the effects of their actions, preferring to leave it to someone else to sort out. In recent decades, these effects have begun to take on global proportions. Like the sorcerer's apprentice, we have unleashed a magic we cannot control. We have unwittingly invented the means to wreak large-scale and irreversible havoc upon our home planet.

Technology will itself change. Even if we were to solve the problems associated with cars or agricultural chemicals, it is likely that new technologies with large-scale environmental effects would come along to take their place. The environmental crisis is to do with how we use technology, how and why we develop technology, and who benefits. Perhaps as it's not the environment that's at fault, we could better describe the environmental crisis as a technological crisis.

However, we can't just blame technology. What about the people who invent, operate, or own the technology? Some environmentalists have condemned the human race in general, likening it to a virus on the face of the planet. Some schools of environmentalist thought have highlighted one simple cause, putting the blame on one group or another by virtue of their class, gender, or nationality.

But is the question of blame even the right one to be asking? The point, as Karl Marx observed, 'philosophers have only interpreted the world in various ways; the point, however, is to change it'.[12] Or, as Siddhartha might have put it, the quest is not to analyse suffering, but to end it. For me, the question is not so much whether any of the different theories of environmentalism are right or wrong, but whether they offer a prospect for change that can actually be realized. In this respect, they all lead, in one way or another, to one challenge – that of human motivation. However change occurs, it will do so because people learn to behave differently. Whatever our analysis of the environmental crisis, and whatever historic causes we choose to emphasize, this challenge cannot be ignored. In the end, it's not an environmental or a technological crisis we're facing: it's a human crisis.

How do you motivate people to change? Or more to the point, how do you even motivate yourself to change? Why should I bother? Why should I take responsibility for other people or for the natural world? How will this make me happier?

Let's return to the figure of Siddhartha leaving the palace. He did so, as we have seen, because he felt hemmed in. The discomfort of leaving the palace and going to live in the wilderness was as nothing compared to the frustration he would have felt if he had stayed. For him, it seems, the desire to help others was as natural as the desire of a lion to roam free. Was Siddhartha fundamentally different to the rest of us in this respect? He himself would say not. He was not a god or a prophet, just an ordinary human being. Is there anything in our own experience that resonates with his sense of being restricted?

You can only answer that question for yourself. I suspect it's a question that takes some thinking about, as we very easily get so used to limitation that we cease to be fully aware of it. I can see it in my own experience in a number of ways, especially in relation to the kind of lifestyle that is portrayed as the norm or the ideal by the media and advertising industry. Because Westernized societies are characterized by high-consumption lifestyles, they give rise to a collective sense of limitation. The flip side of materialism is boredom, anxiety, and guilt.

Boredom arises when we believe the message we are given that possessions – houses, cars, computers – will ultimately make us happy. This can lead us to invest too much of our hopes of happiness in the wrong things. In Britain, people make fun of train-spotters, but is this so different from getting hung up about different models of car or other kinds of gadgetry? Sooner or later, we grow bored and want the upgraded model. These are no more likely to give us lasting satisfaction than the number on the side of a railway engine.

In the wake of boredom comes anxiety. We have to spend time, money, and mental energy keeping up the payments on our possessions: protecting them, insuring them, and so on. In the background lies the knowledge that the whole economic system that supports Western lifestyles has to be protected by huge military forces. I clearly remember my primary school teacher telling us for the first time about nuclear weapons.

It marked the arrival of a dull sense of anxiety that, notwithstanding the end of the Cold War, has never gone away. I suspect we are all so used to anxiety that we have come to think of it as normal.

Guilt arises because, despite our sophisticated attempts to ignore it, we know instinctively that there is some connection between our high-consumption lifestyles and poverty and environmental degradation. We know that we could do more to alleviate poverty. We know the rubbish we carelessly throw away has to go somewhere. We know that exhaust fumes pollute the air. In ordinary, everyday actions, we are adding to the residue of guilt. We are alienating ourselves from humanity and the natural world.

Boredom, anxiety, and guilt: these three poisons of materialist societies imprison us to an extent we're probably not aware of. To the extent that we have succeeded in relegating them to the edge of our consciousness, we have become comfortably numb. They prevent us from having a happy and straightforward relationship with other people and with the world around us.

So to continue our search for causes, what are the causes of boredom, anxiety, and guilt? How did we come to imprison ourselves so? How do we become free?

Waking up

Siddhartha Gautama, living in a forest 2,500 years ago, asked himself exactly such questions. Having sought out the most renowned spiritual teachers of his time, he learned how to meditate and how to try to break through to the meaning of life through extreme physical hardships and fasting. He gained a reputation as an ascetic himself. In time, though, he saw that

such extremes of austerity weren't helping him at all and that
he was no nearer to finding the answers to his questions.

Sensing that a middle way would be a more fruitful
approach, he started eating moderately again and embarked
on a period of deep meditation. It was in the course of this
that, sitting beneath a tree, he found that he was able to let
go of the very last vestiges of greed, hatred, and unawareness. He had let go, once and for all, of seeing reality from a
self-centred point of view. Hardly daring to believe that he
had reached the end of his quest, he reached out his right
hand and gently touched the earth with the tips of his fingers.
As if the earth itself confirmed the reality of what had happened, his last remaining doubt evaporated. He experienced
perfect clarity of mind, which was naturally accompanied
by unbounded compassion for all living things. This was the
awakening of his heart and mind to a state of utter peace and
freedom from suffering. From then on, he became known as
the Buddha, the ` Awakened One'.

According to the most accurate description he could give
within the constraints of language, the key to the Buddha's
liberation was the profound significance and reality of change.
This was expressed in that part of his teaching often referred
to as conditioned co-production: that everything that goes on
in the universe is a constant flow of interdependent networks
of causes and effects. Every single thing, on every level, from
the smallest to the grandest scale, from second to second and
aeon to aeon, comes about on the basis of a set of conditions.
Take away the conditions, and it ceases to exist. As a result,
nothing is immune from change. Ultimately, everything
affects everything else.

Why is this so radical and important? From our limited
points of view, we want to believe that we are always going to

be here in our present form and that things are always going to be the way we want them. Reality constantly reminds us that this is not the case. The world changes faster than we are comfortable with. We ourselves change from one day to the next, from one second to the next. Our moods, our thoughts, our bodies are in constant flux. For all of us there exists the ever-present prospect of disease, old age, and death. But we do our best to ignore it. We might see intellectually that everything is subject to change, but we don't accept it emotionally.

We try to grasp things that we think will give us permanent satisfaction. And if something or somebody gets in the way, we can react with aversion. Thus our stubborn unawareness of change is bound up with greed, hatred, fear, and anxiety. These are, in turn, bound up with suffering because, at heart, they represent a tension between reality and us.

The environmental crisis arises from the same tension. We want to believe that the natural world is so expansive that we can treat it as we wish without fear of the consequences. We want to believe that problems will be sorted out without any effort or sacrifice on our part. We want to carry on buying things without thinking about the effects on other people. We want to believe that there are unlimited sources of energy, clean water, and food. We want to believe that the sky is big enough to take all our pollution. For all its social, economic, and scientific complexity, what the environmental crisis boils down to is greed, hatred, and unawareness. These are the roots of boredom, anxiety, and guilt.

To let go of these fantasies would require us to make difficult decisions that we'd rather not face up to, so the fantasies are self-perpetuating. Greed, hatred, and unawareness are habits by which we limit our own happiness and freedom. Like any habit, they take time to let go of, but over time we can learn to let go of the idea that the me 'in here' is ultimately separate and different from other people and the universe 'out there'. We can experience ourselves as part of nature. We can become more compassionate, and, as there is no fixed law saying that particular beings have to experience a given amount of misery, we are free to become happier. In fact, there is no limit to how happy we are allowed to become – all we need is the means to do so. The world does not have to be in the state it is. Change is possible.

Imagine a world freed from poverty, war, and pollution. Never mind, for a moment, whether or not this is impossible idealism. Imagine the sense of joy and relief. It would be like a thousand Berlin walls collapsing.

If that's too difficult, imagine yourself on your deathbed, looking back on your life. Imagine you've made some effort to change things, to live in greater harmony with others and with nature. The world's problems may not be solved, but you know in your heart that you've done what you could to make the world a better place. Compare that to how you'd feel if you knew you'd gone on being part of the problem, blindly hoping that someone else would sort out the mess.

Individually, we need to wake up from our habits of greed, hatred, and unawareness. Collectively, we need to wake up from our boredom, anxiety, and guilt. But is such change really possible? How could it come about? Even if I could change myself, surely that would not be enough. How do I change the world as well?

Changing ourselves

The Buddha saw the vast potential range of the human condition. The same species that can degrade its home planet can also devote itself to saving it. The same goes for individuals. We often blind ourselves to this. We often demonize some people and sanctify others, as if we want to put them in a separate category from ourselves. We think of people as saints or messiahs, or monsters possessed by some special evil. The Buddha had a less fixed view of what and who we are. He taught that, in each second, with everything that we do, think, and say, we are shaping ourselves. We become what we do. With every act of greed, hatred, or unawareness, we develop qualities of selfishness and narrow-mindedness. With every act of love and kindness, we develop qualities of empathy and clarity. If we do any of these consistently enough, we can become greedy destroyers or bringers of peace. There are no limits, and everyone is free to change.

In Buddhism, the human state is regarded as immensely precious, precisely because it offers the potential for further development. The Buddha taught that this potential is limitless, that wisdom and compassion have no bounds. However much we already have these qualities, there are always new horizons. Each new day is an opportunity to explore our potential further. Complacency and moral superiority only distract us from the journey.

The Buddha set out a very practical path by which we can progressively liberate ourselves from our self-limiting habits. It includes meditation, together with a way of training ourselves to behave towards the world with non-violence and more loving-kindness. I'll say more about this later.

Changing the world

Looked at in the broader sweep of history, humankind has reached a crossroads. The long process of biological and mental evolution has endowed us with the capacity for a high degree of self-awareness. At some point, natural selection conferred a survival advantage on those primates with a greater capacity for introspection, probably because it helped to predict the behaviour of others. Since then, we have been able to imagine what it might be like to be someone else and how they might view us.[13] We have become the universe aware of itself.

Whether we use this capacity for self-awareness and empathy is up to us. Our experience of it is often sporadic. Some days we feel clearer and kinder than on other days. It has also waxed and waned through history. Some cultures have prized and developed it, whereas others have neglected it. Those that have valued it tend towards civilization and co-operation, while those that have neglected it tend towards exploitation and control. The choice we face now may be very stark indeed – between a leap forward in the cultivation of awareness on the one hand and self-inflicted extinction on the other.

Some people think that Buddhism is just a path to individual peace of mind, a selfish escape from the realities of the world. This could hardly be further from the truth; the Buddha taught that real happiness comes from waking up to how we are connected with others. His teachings help us to find greater happiness not only for ourselves, but also for others. The two go together. They give us the means not only to change ourselves, but also to change the world.

Realizing that he had found the path to end the suffering of human existence, the Buddha devoted the rest of his life to helping others to follow in his footsteps. Cutting across the boundaries of caste and gender, he walked from place to place in northern India, teaching and befriending beggars, kings, warriors, courtesans, murderers, and priests. There are many stories about these encounters; the picture that emerges is one of a man without any of the affectations of a pseudo-spiritual teacher, without glibness or pride. He did not consider himself above helping a sick disciple. He had an intuitive understanding of people which enabled him to communicate with them in whatever way was appropriate – gentle words, blunt directness, rational argument, or a kindly, ironic humour. By the time he passed away, aged about eighty, he had followers from all sections of society across northern India, and he had started a spiritual tradition that was to spread down the centuries and across the world.

The Buddha not only inspired individual men and women, but, as a natural consequence, the society in which he lived. His world was dominated by the caste system, which condemned many people to demeaning servitude from birth until death. The Buddha refused to have anything to do with caste, and urged his followers to do likewise.[14] The effect of this was that, as his teachings spread, many people liberated themselves from caste. Even in contemporary India, a revival of the Buddha's teachings has given new hope and self-respect to millions of people formerly regarded as being of the lowest, so-called 'Untouchable', Hindu caste. The Buddha exerted this influence on history not by trying to take control of society, but by uncompromisingly exemplifying a more positive ideal.

The Buddha's teachings offer a practical means to unlock our own potential for changing the world. This is why they have so much to offer the environmental movement at this point in its history. Environmentalists have achieved successes in the last fifty years or so on a heroic scale. They have established worldwide campaigning organizations, they have brought issues to the public's attention, they have educated people in how to begin to make things better by changing their own lives. They have brought ideas such as sustainable development (development that meets present-day needs without compromising the ability of future generations to meet theirs) into schools, boardrooms, and the corridors of power.

But many environmentalists now feel they are coming up against the brick walls of political inertia and entrenched economic interest. Attempts to reach international agreement on the reduction of carbon emissions have been slow and incomplete. Government decisions have been taken in the short-term profit-making interests of large corporations rather than in the long-term interest of the common good. Increasingly, the big environmental issues are bound up with the global disparities of wealth and power. The writer Tom Athanasiou has remarked that the fundamental political truth of our time is that the change that is necessary is not 'realistic'. That is to say, it is not regarded as realistic.[15] While many people understand the need for change, bringing it about is another matter. The environmental movement is becoming aware of this as its new priority. It is not enough to alert the public to the facts; somehow we need to motivate them to act. As a former director of Greenpeace puts it, 'We know that the world is burning. The question is how to put out the fire.'[16]

Awakening hearts and minds: the Bodhisattva path

What we need is a way of not only waking ourselves from our self-limiting habits, but also waking the rest of the world from fixed ways of thinking. It needs to be a practical path rather than a distant ideology. It needs to end in what seem to be impossible dreams of world harmony and a clean planet, but it needs to begin where we are now, with all our doubts and imperfections.

Saving the Earth

The process of awakening the heart and mind is such a path. One of the names accorded to it by the Buddhist tradition is the path of the Bodhisattva. A Bodhisattva is 'one who strives for awakening' not merely for his or her own sake but for the sake of all living beings. As an ideal, the Bodhisattva is often portrayed as the epitome of altruism, utterly dedicated to the welfare of the world.

Ideals can sometimes seem a very long way off, but anyone can begin to be a Bodhisattva. The Bodhisattva path – the path of learning and awakening – can start anywhere. It promises greater happiness on the most humble as well as the most elevated level, and it requires no blind faith in some distant ideal. It consists in the steady cultivation of the qualities of generosity, ethical conduct, patience, energy, meditation, and wisdom.[17] We will explore each of these in the next few chapters.

As well as being a way to greater personal happiness, the Bodhisattva path offers a way to equip ourselves for the task of effectively addressing the environmental crisis. It is a way of training ourselves in the qualities we will need if we are really going to make a difference.

3

Only Connect!

IMAGINE YOU ARE TRAVELLING SOMEWHERE BY SHIP. You are below decks and suddenly, the alarms sound, the lights go out, the vessel lurches severely to one side and begins to fill with water. What is your first reaction? Is it to immediately look for an escape route, and start scrambling up gangways to the decks to find a lifeboat? Or might it be that you first look around to see who is there with you, and then begin to cooperate so that you all find a way out, perhaps making sure that anyone weaker or more vulnerable gets out ahead of you?

Maybe we'll never really know the answer to that unless we find ourselves in a similar situation. But the predicament tells us a lot about human nature. Some researchers have interviewed a large number of people who have survived disasters at sea.[18] They found that those who had survived by cooperating with others were much better able to return happily to their lives. Those who had survived by going it alone were much more likely to suffer long-term trauma from their ordeal. This was borne out in a recent interview with a man who had survived the sinking of a ferry some years ago, in which hundreds people had died. He said that every day he still felt haunted by the fact that he had not stopped to help other people to safety.

I find this both fascinating and moving, because it points to something at the very heart of who we are as human beings. It is in our deepest nature to connect with those around us. If we do anything to deny that connection, we are bound, sooner or later, to feel the pain of it in some way.

So perhaps our first response to environmental crisis should not just be to think about how we impact on nature, but rather to look around and see who is there with us.

Living in harmony with nature is inseparable from living in harmony with each other. It's not just a question of somehow bolting environmental awareness on to our existing lifestyles. Environmental problems, with their roots in greed, hatred, and unawareness, should cause us to question our whole way of being in the world. When the Buddha saw that we are not ultimately separate from the universe or from others, it was not just an intellectual observation. His realization that all things are interconnected was something felt in his heart as much as his head, and it moved him to live out the rest of his life helping others.

In the Buddhist scriptures, there is a story about three disciples of the Buddha who were living in a wooded place called Gosinga.[19] One day, the Buddha came to visit. He first enquired after their physical well-being and then asked whether they were living together in harmony. He was pleased to find that they were bearing each other in mind so naturally that no words about practical tasks were needed. The first to return from the alms round would fetch drinking water, and the last would wash the refuse bucket. Whoever noticed that the washing water was low would fetch more. Each would maintain the attitude that while they were different in body, they were one in mind. Being sensitive to nature, they took care that no waste was discarded wherever there was greenery or water that supported life. For the three disciples, devoted to simplicity and meditation, complete harmony with each other and with their environment was the foundation of a truly human existence.

If we experience a desire to do something to help the environment, it is probably because we ourselves have to some extent understood interconnectedness. According to the Buddha, this is something we can grow to understand more and more deeply. We can do this by trying it out, little by little, through individual acts of kindness. If we are truly interconnected, these will make us on the whole freer and happier. In the rest of this chapter, I'd like to examine how this sense of exploration might bring to life our whole approach to the environment.

The armchair society

In the West, people have become ever more oriented to material consumption, and live in smaller and smaller units. The average number of people in each household is steadily declining. If the trends continue much further, we will soon all be sitting in our own armchair, in our own house, watching our own television. The information age, progressing through the successive technologies of radio, television, the internet, and mobile phones, is reaching the point of saturation, where everyone has instant access to virtually unlimited information. We have televisions in the kitchen and the bedroom, computers on our palms, and telephones in our pockets. In turn, each new technology has become the object of fetishistic desire, as a status symbol or fashion statement. All too often, the actual content of the information having been transmitted, the quality of our communication becomes of secondary or no importance at all. Indeed, the very quantity of information at our fingertips can numb our minds to the whole notion of quality. The television addict, the computer nerd, and the loud but vacuous mobile phone user have become the successive icons of the passing decades.

It is not just information that we expect to have at our command. We expect fast food, fast transport, fast service. We expect a wide array of choices of even the most everyday products. I heard a story of an East European woman who was visiting England. Faced with the bewildering array of different kinds of shampoo on a supermarket shelf, she burst into tears. Yet choice is what we've come to expect and consider normal. We would probably like to think of ourselves as an exception – it's other people who are the rampant materialists, who are obsessed with information and gadgets. But I wonder whether it might apply to all of us more than we'd like to acknowledge. When you are brought up within a particular culture, you unconsciously imbibe its values and habits. We can come to consider the strangest things quite normal.

The writer Helena Norberg-Hodge lived for many years in the Himalayan kingdom of Ladakh. It is a place that had, until the advent of the Westernized economy, a very strong sense of community and co-operation. Despite living in a land with few resources and a harsh climate, Ladakhis have a reputation for irrepressible happiness and laughter. Norberg-Hodge relates how, when told that many people in the affluent West were so unhappy they had to go to see their doctor, the Ladakhis' mouths dropped open in astonishment.[20]

How have we so spectacularly failed to build a happy society despite our material wealth? How can we begin to move forward? What are the unconscious assumptions that are holding us back?

We carry a model in our heads about the way we function in society, one that most of us rarely question. We see ourselves as tightly defined units, either individually or in households. To put it crudely, money comes into the unit at one end when we receive our wages and it goes out of the other when we buy things. Compared to other societies, our actual experience of being connected with others is slight. The advertising industry, which equates consumption with status, and the job market both promote an essentially competitive relationship between units. Somewhere along the line we have lost the art of living together.

In the post-industrial era, many of the cohesive forces in society have been weakened. There is much more geographical and social mobility. There are few who live and work with the same people, and families and friends tend to live further apart. Traditional rural communities and industrial working-class neighbourhoods have largely dispersed. There are few communities left where a unifying ideology, such as Christianity, socialism, or nationalism, can be taken for granted. The ideal of democracy, in so far as it is shared, allows us to live together but does not necessarily provide a common purpose, something higher than our private economic interests.

Our problem is that we are living as though disconnected. We think we are disconnected from our neighbours, from people in other countries, from the natural world. But this isn't in accord with reality. It just doesn't work. Everything we eat and drink comes from the earth. We depend on others in countless ways even for the most basic necessities of life. But, too often, we just want to look after our own little unit. And the more we have withdrawn into our own private sphere, the more boredom, loneliness, or desire for status has driven us to consume.

We now have a choice. One option is to sit in our armchair and accept the ascendancy of untrammelled capitalism, with all its social and environmental problems. Another is to try to escape to an imagined utopia away from it all, a rustic idyll where we can turn back the clock. A third option is to begin to build within our society a new cohesion, co-operation, and trust from first principles, based not on an imposed ideology but on our common humanity. This means patiently beginning the work of rebuilding. It means connecting with people, as a way of trying out the truth of interconnectedness.

To begin this patient work of rebuilding, we can reflect on how we affect other people individually and on how we affect the world as a whole. Having done so, we can make a conscious effort to connect with people in a more positive way by giving.

How do I affect other people?

Every time you speak to someone, buy something from them, or just sit opposite them on a train, you are sending out ripples of cause and effect into the world. The effects are sometimes positive, sometimes negative. Being preoccupied with our own concerns, we all too often forget this, but as part of the process of learning and awakening, we can train ourselves to think more about it. I'll come back to this later. The point I want to make here is that it's not just our deliberately willed actions that affect others. We are constantly communicating with others across a much broader spectrum than simply our words. Through every minor detail of our body and speech, we communicate who we are as well as what we do. We communicate our lifestyle, our state of mind, our values. The Vietnamese monk Thich Nhat Hanh illustrates this with another example of people in peril on the sea – some refugee 'boat people'adrift on a small vessel:

Often the boats are caught in rough seas or storms, the people may panic, and boats can sink. But if even one person aboard can remain calm, lucid, knowing what to do and what not to do, he or she can help the boat survive. His or her expression – face, voice – communicates clarity and calmness, and people have trust in that person. They will listen to what he or she says. One such person can save the lives of many. [21]

When we talk with other people about environmental issues or the state of the world, it is not just what we are saying that makes a difference, but how we are saying it. We can communicate panic and despair, or clarity and calm. The communication of panic and despair follows from a desire to take from other people a sense of reassurance or comfort. The communication of clarity and calm follows from a desire to work with others to find a solution. These are two very different kinds of environmentalism.

We can see this even in very ordinary circumstances. If you have ever worked with someone in a very negative state of mind, you will know how this casts a cloud over everyone. Conversely, just the occasional friendly word on a train can dispel the atmosphere of reserve and make for a more relaxed and enjoyable journey for everyone.

This certainly isn't to say that political activity isn't necessary, but we shouldn't lose sight of how we affect people in very ordinary ways. Having high ideals about saving the environment is not necessarily enough; one could spend one's whole life talking and thinking about ideas, bold plans, utopian visions, but without a way of putting them into practice, at least to some extent, they have not necessarily been the slightest bit of use to anybody. There is a danger with big issues such as the global environment that you lose yourself in abstractions. You might even entertain private fantasies about saving the world single-handedly. You can convince yourself that you have great concern for the world, when actually you can't even get along with the people you see every day.

A sharing revolution

What are the ordinary individual words and deeds that will bring about a phase transition towards an environmentally sustainable future? If lack of connection lies at the heart of the problem, it follows that the most direct antidotes are things that start to reconnect us, such as giving and sharing. The quality of generosity is rarely mentioned in environmentalist writings, yet it has never been so indispensable. Giving material things reminds us that happiness comes from connecting with others. Sharing things breaks down the barriers of our isolated consumer units.

Giving and sharing are powerful acts because they undermine the notion, taken for granted by some economists, that we all act out of economic self-interest and that economic growth is the greatest good. On a world scale, these qualities will be expressed as a global vision of fairness and security, which will counter the attitude, still advanced by leading politicians, that the national economic interest should always take precedence over global concerns. Economists can only measure financial transactions and too easily forget that happiness does not equate with how much money we spend.[22]

Generosity is a kind of liberation movement. Liberation movements arise when people refuse to assent any longer to whatever regime or ideology is oppressing them. The idea of freedom becomes contagious and pressure for change becomes irresistible. If materialism and isolation are the great oppressions of Western society, then generosity is liberation.

So the first step forward can be taken through the very ordinary and simple act of generosity. Anyone can do it. Even someone in the most self-absorbed state, if they put their mind to it, can find some way of giving, even if it's just a tiny gesture of friendliness. This is the first step towards rejoining the human race, connecting with others. It relieves us from the narrow, constricted pain of selfish isolation.

Progressively, starting from wherever we are and working outwards, we can try out more ways of freeing ourselves. At each stage, we can reflect on how generosity feels, not in a self-righteous way, but feeling what it's like to be more connected to other human beings. If you have ever worked in a situation where everyone is pulling together, or played in a band, or been part of a sports team, you may recall sometimes thinking in terms of 'us' rather than 'me'. We can look to develop this sense of 'us-ness' in our everyday lives, beginning with those around us, then including more and more people. Here are some examples of giving and sharing, many of which have an environmental flavour:

- Give a gift to your neighbour.
- Pick up a piece of litter every day.
- Share garden tools.
- Start a car-sharing scheme.
- Adopt a development charity to give to, or volunteer for.
- Offer your services via a local or international volunteer bureau.[23]
- Adopt a local green space and help to improve it.

- Become a conservation volunteer.[24]
- Join a LETS (Local Exchange Trading Scheme) or a skills co-operative.[25]

There are many other things we could do, of course. Perhaps as we go on, we'll find that these sort of changes enrich our lives and we want to increase the amount of time and energy we give to them. This is one way of responding to the environmental crisis – learning to connect with others more and more. A sharing society will tend to live in greater harmony with nature.

A reflection

Take some time to reflect on what you communicate to others, how you connect to others across this broad bandwidth through your body language and tone of voice. You may be fortunate and know someone whom you could ask and who will give you an honest answer.

Consider in particular whether you transmit calm or anxiety, clarity or confusion, friendliness, reserve, or ill will. Communicate a natural concern when talking about environmental issues, rather than despair. Think back to people who have had a positive influence on your life. What was it about their communication that affected you? Could you affect others in a similar way?

How do I change the world?

As well as thinking we are disconnected from others, we very often think we are disconnected from the world at large. To use the words of the political thinker André Gorz, we feel 'impotent in the face of autonomized processes and face-less powers'.[26] We tend to think that the world is only really changed by people in positions of wealth and power. This is certainly the view perpetrated by the news media, which can often whip up the most trivial murmur in circles of govern-ment as if it were a matter of great national import.

But this is a very narrow way of thinking about how change occurs, and one that makes us feel so marginal and unimportant that we can be misled into thinking that our own actions don't have consequences. An alternative view is that acts of parliament or international treaties come about because of the forces of public opinion, or perhaps something deeper than just opinion. People's values and perceptions, individually and collectively, can shift in quite mysterious and unpredictable ways. The sum total of the broad bandwidth of communications going on, by which people communicate their values and states of mind, will have an effect. In this light, formal politics can look more like what the writer Tor Nørretranders has described as 'tardy rationalizations of what has already taken place'.[27] He cites as an example the end of the mutual paranoia that underpinned the Cold War. In the mid-1980s, he argues, even before the break-up of the Soviet bloc, there was a defusing of tension that could not be explained by any formal political process. He speculates that this was the result of millions of ordinary people, persistently, over the decades, talking about the unthinkable nature of nuclear war. In unseen ways, they brought about a phase transition that changed history. In this perspective, politicians just bumble along a few years behind the cutting edge of change. Human society is as complex and chaotic as any ecosystem. We may think that our behaviour, conversations, and transactions are our own private business, but, in aggregate, they are constantly bringing about changes in ways we don't even suspect. You don't have to win an election or stage a revolution to change the world. Our actions do have consequences.

Together we are more

The Buddhist writer and activist Joanna Macy has spent many years helping people to overcome despair about the state of the world and realize that their actions do matter. I recall that, while discussing this with a group of which I was part, she was talking about the predicament that many of us find ourselves in. We see the extent and global scale of problems in the world, and from that we get an idea of the sheer enormity of the resources that would be needed to turn things around. Then we look inside ourselves and see that our own personal qualities and strengths are pitifully inadequate to the task. How can I possibly change the world? At this point in the discussion, she said something that quite took me by surprise. 'The good news is,' she said, 'you don't have to.'

The root of the problem, here again, is that we think of ourselves in isolation – little me 'in here' trying to change the big world 'out there'. As long as we keep that mindset, we're stuck. Joanna was making the point that the strengths and qualities needed to make a difference in the world aren't going to arise within any one individual. They arise between us, when we come together and unite in a higher cause.

That insight came as an immense relief. Like many of us, I'd been stuck to some extent in the mindset of 'me' trying to save 'the world'. To let go of that felt like the weight of the world being lifted from my shoulders. Which, indeed, it was.

Only Connect!

So this is another reason why we need to look around and see who is there with us. Not only is it in our deepest nature to connect with others, but it is also in so doing that we, together, tap into strengths and resources that are quite beyond us as individuals.

The great turning

Joanna Macy and others have referred to a network of this kind as the 'Great Turning'. The term includes all those communities that have arisen independently in response to the current ecological crisis, and which operate in harmony with others and with the natural environment. With sufficient vitality, this could bring about an epochal shift from a society based on industrial and economic growth to one based on sustaining life.

From high school students restoring streams for salmon spawning, to inner city neighbours creating community gardens on vacant lots, from forest activists sitting in trees to delay logging until environmental impact studies are done, to windmill engineers bringing their technology to energy-hungry regions – countless groups are organizing, learning, taking action. This multifaceted activity on behalf of life may not make today's headlines or newscasts, but to our progeny it will matter more than anything else we do.[28]

The 'Great Turning' involves three related areas of activity.

1. Holding actions that try to limit the damage to the natural world and living systems, such as preventing pollution or mitigating its effects

2. Analysing the causes of the ecological crisis and creating alternatives, such as community gardens, co-operative housing and environmentally sustainable technologies
3. Bringing about a cognitive and spiritual shift in perceptions based on an understanding of the interconnectedness of living systems and the natural world

Sangharakshita makes a similar point. The essence of a Buddhist approach to current world problems, he says, is that we act in community, in this case in 'spiritual communities', or communities that support the development of individuals. We should act not so much as kings of the jungle as indefatigable earthworms.

If enough earthworms burrow away under the foundations of even the most substantial building, the soil begins to loosen, it starts to crumble away, the foundations subside, and the whole building is liable to crack and collapse. Likewise, however powerful the existing order may seem, it is not invulnerable to the undermining influence of enough individuals working – whether directly or indirectly – in co-operation.

A spiritual community is necessarily small, so the best we can hope for is a multiplicity of spiritual communities, forming a sort of network through personal contact between their members. A silent, unseen influence is exerted in this way, which we must hope will be able, at some point, to shift the centre of gravity in world affairs from the conflict of groups to the co-operation of communities. If this were achieved, if the influence of the spiritual community were to outweigh that of the group, then humanity as a whole would have passed into a new, higher stage of development, a kind of higher evolution as I like to call it.

Such a shift in the governing values of the world is probably all that can save us from extinction as a species in the not very distant future. There are certainly signs of hope, but there is also perhaps little time left. In this situation it becomes the duty of every thinking human being to take stock of his or her position, and the responsibilities that it throws up. We have to appreciate that it is, without exception, the most important issue we shall ever face, either individually or collectively. It is certainly more important than any merely religious question, anything that concerns Buddhism in the sense of a formal or established religion. It concerns both the purpose and the very survival of human life. [29]

So our first task is to connect with others. We need to so because it is painful and limiting to do otherwise. We need to do so, because it is the most direct way of healing a disconnected world. And we need to do so because it is in connection with others that we find the strength we need to bring about change.

This was true even for the Buddha himself. After his awakening, he surveyed the suffering of the world and was moved to devote his whole life to ending it. His first act was then to look around and see who was there with him. He sought out those who were most likely to share his vision and understanding. He found five of his former disciples, who in turn became awakened and shared in his task. In that first simple act, the Buddha founded a community that has embraced many millions of people and continues as an influence for good in the world to this day. In our generation, more than ever, the world needs us to come fully alive to ourselves and connect generously and joyfully with all those who are there with us.

4

Love, Love, Love

IN THIS CHAPTER, I WILL BE LOOKING at some of the lifestyle changes we might think about making to protect the environment. There is an abundance of books and websites offering all kinds of advice, often in the form of lists of do's and don'ts. I'll come to some of these practical matters later on, but first let's go back to basics and ask why we might want to make the changes in the first place.

Motivation really matters. Sometimes we can make changes out of a dry sense of duty, or because we fear the disapproval of our more 'environmentally correct' friends. Lists of do's and don'ts can too easily be treated as lists of rules. The problem of following rules is that you can forget the original motivation for doing so and it becomes a very dry experience. There's a danger of becoming a bit of an eco-bore. You've probably met the kind of person who sternly tells you off for putting your orange peel in the wrong compost bin. Or worse, you might have found yourself doing it to others. This probably does more harm than good. How many of us are so perfect that we are in a position to judge others? In any case, what is an easy decision for us might require a real effort for someone else. A morally superior attitude really fails to inspire other people to take action. Perhaps the best thing to do if you find it creeping into your own thinking is to throw your jam jars into the main rubbish bin for a day or two, and enjoy the sense of freedom!

Buddhism doesn't generally advocate rules and commandments, so on our path of 'Buddhism as environmentalism', we'll need to find another approach.

What Buddhism does have is precepts. These are training principles that help us to cultivate clear and positive states of mind. The most basic set of five encourage us to cultivate:

- acts of loving-kindness,

- open-handed generosity,

- stillness, simplicity, and contentment,

- truthful communication, and

- clear and radiant awareness.

The precepts are a very down-to-earth and practical set of guidelines. The vast majority of our actions aren't determined by imposed sets of rules, but by our emotions and states of mind. Even if we do follow rules against our deeper wishes, our emotions will probably find a way of rebelling somewhere along the line. So the precepts are very realistic. If we want to make true and lasting change, it is our states of mind and our motivation that we need to attend to.

What underlies the precepts is a basic desire that other beings should not come to harm. They are guidelines to help us cultivate non-violent and loving states of mind. The Buddha himself exemplified non-violence. Not only did he oppose the iniquities of the caste system of his day, but he also repeatedly spoke against the practice of blood sacrifice.[30] There is some evidence that the Buddha's teachings brought about a change of attitude towards animals throughout India, even within his own lifetime, which endures today.[31] Non-violence is difficult or even impossible to apply in an absolute way. Just being alive implicates us in the death of countless micro-organisms inside our bodies. There are many situations in the world – violent crime, state brutality, terrorism, war – in which it is hard to see a non-violent solution that does not itself imply more suffering. But these difficulties need not deter us from being as non-violent as we can, trying our best in each circumstance to see the best way forward. They don't undermine non-violence as a principle, but only go to demonstrate that we live in a world of complex choices, where we don't have the comfort of simplistic rules that will tell us what to do in every situation.

What we can do, over a period of time, is push back the boundaries of our sensitivity to other living things. In Buddhist ethics, what defines an act as positive or negative is not whether it conforms to a rule, but the motivation behind it. So non-violence is not a rule or an external observance, but a state of heart and mind. In each situation, we bring to bear whatever wisdom and compassion we have and try to act non-violently. From each situation, we learn how we might have done better, how we can become wiser and more compassionate. The Buddha likened this development of wisdom and compassion to lotuses growing from the mud. We may begin by being tightly closed and bound within mud, but we can start to reach out of the mud and up through the water. Eventually, we will rise above the surface of the pond and open up to the sunlight as beautifully coloured and fragrant flowers.

Love, Love, Love

The fact that Buddhism isn't about rules doesn't mean that effort is not required. Nowadays, the complexities of manufacturing systems, technological processes, and trading patterns all obscure from us the effects of our actions. We don't know where our potatoes were grown, which forest our newspaper came from. We don't see the undesired effects of the chemicals we spray in our gardens. We may not even know what happens to our own effluent once we flush it away.

It follows that to act truly ethically in the modern world will require some extra effort on our part. The changes we need to make to our lives are very real and visible, while the benefits they might have are far away and far removed. It is very easy in these circumstances to develop ethical blind spots – areas that we're dimly aware of but would rather not look into too closely. But if we do look at them, they can be seen as valuable opportunities, because these are exactly the changes that will have the most transformative effect on ourselves and consequently the world.

We need to be willing to change our habits. People often fear that behaving in an environmentally friendly way means spending one's days lost in complex calculations of the effects of car exhausts, roof lagging, and plastic bags, continually weighing one course of action against another. But our lifestyles are really just an amalgam of habits. We don't usually decide from scratch on each new occasion which washing powder to buy or how to travel to work. With a little initial effort, habits can be changed. Perhaps we can have the greatest effect by keeping the environment in mind when making big decisions – where to live, how to make a living, where to go on holiday, and so on.

The two precepts that seem most relevant to the kind of practical lifestyle changes we're looking at here are the first and third (the others are covered in other chapters). Loving kindness, or non-violence, is at the very heart of Buddhist practice. Sometimes people ask me what Buddhism has to do with issues like climate change. Well, they could read all the books and articles on the subject, but really all they need to look at is that first precept. Simplicity is also at the very heart of Buddhism (it has a big heart!), as exemplified by the Buddha himself.

Let us look further at the spirit of those two precepts, in turn, and what they might have to do with environmental issues.

Falling in love again

Even when Buddhism praises deeds of loving kindness, you can get the idea that it's saying that there are certain 'good deeds' that a good Buddhist 'ought' to do. But let us not overlook the verb 'loving' in the precept. Buddhism is about coming alive. Buddhism as environmentalism isn't about doing good; it's about actual heart-felt, gut-felt love.

In recent times, we've come to think of our environment as basically consisting of inanimate matter. Science has in many ways greatly extended our understanding of the world. But, especially in the nineteenth and early twentieth centuries, it also tended to reduce everything to lifeless particles. The environment then becomes a thing we happen to live in and draw resources from and throw away our unwanted things into. It's very hard to really love something that we don't think of as being alive.

One of the roots of the environmental crisis is that we've become disenchanted with the places we live in. In traditional societies, nature is seen as alive. It may be personified in the form of spirits and gods, or seen as an impersonal creative force that infuses the natural world. Words for this kind of force are found in many indigenous cultures – the 'Ramat' of the Ainu in northern Japan; the 'Mana' of Melanesia; the 'Wakon' of the Dakota and the 'Orenda' of the Ironquois, both native American tribes. However you conceive of it, or whatever name you give it, the point is that nature becomes something that you can feel a heart connection with. You can love nature, and nature can love you back.

To our post-industrial society, nature is like a neglected and long-lost lover, and one who, perhaps we are just beginning to realize, we cannot live without.[32] Somehow we need to find a way to reach out, heal the hurt, and fall back in love again.

So how do long-lost lovers fall in love again? Maybe it begins in small ways – a glance, a smile, tender words, little gestures or tokens of affection. From those, other things might develop – reconciliation, a deeper, enduring connection, and living together in harmony.

'Nature' and 'the environment' are quite abstract words. What we really mean, of course, when we use those words is trees, rivers, oceans, clouds, birds, fish, insects, and so on. And more than those things viewed individually. Nature, too, is more than the sum of its parts. All those parts of nature combine into intricate ecosystems. They make up places – the forests, reefs, grasslands, and deserts of the world. And they make up the whole delicate web of life that gives the Earth the blue-green iridescence that can be seen from space.

We don't love in abstraction; we love in particular. We love because we feel connected, that in some ways we are one. We can love the earth for feeding our bodies; we can love the rivers and oceans because, in truth, they are not different from the blood that runs through our veins; we can love the air because it sustains us in each breath. If we love something or someone, we won't treat them as mere objects, or as commodities to be traded in complex international treaties. Rather, even if it causes us difficulty and pain, we will do everything we can to cherish and protect them.

Feel local, act global

If the idea of loving physical elements is still too abstract for us, we can love the particular places – the rivers or lakes that we know, the trees in our parks, the birds in our gardens, the wild places we go to to get away from it all.

A few summers ago, I went swimming in the North Sea. It's usually far too cold to stay in for very long, but it was a hot day and it was a gently sloping beach. While relaxing in the unusually warm water, I had a very strong sense that I was surrounded not by dead water, but by a living system. I was brought up next to the North Sea – it's where I paddled as a child – and I still live nearby. But I realized that I'd always just thought of it as an expanse of water. Since that time, I've found myself quite naturally taking more of an interest in the North Sea. I've learnt that its bird life is severely stressed. Because of climate change, the pattern of water currents is changing and unpredictable, The puffin colonies on the Farne Islands off of Northumberland, England have sharply declined, probably because the sand eels they normally eat aren't where they expect to find them. I also took some classes in coastal ecology and learnt that there is an amazingly colourful and diverse reef just off the Northumberland coast. Now, I take a bit more care what I pour down the drain, and I've written to my MP to ask him to support the declaration of a Marine Nature Reserve in the

North Sea. And, because I still love swimming in the sea, I've taken up surfing,

People are nature too

Our lifestyles not only affect nature, but other people too. Very often, in today's complex world, the effects are felt by people far away, in distance or in time. It is relatively easy to be moved to action when we know the people concerned. But it is rather more difficult to feel the same motivation for those far away. Bring to mind, for example, the people who live next door to you. Now imagine that every time you use too much electricity, or book a flight, it floods their home and destroys their livelihood.

So somehow we need to fall in love, in a way, with people we will never meet, and with future generations too.

His Holiness the Dalai Lama talks about the need for 'universal responsibility'.[33] The kind of responsibility he is talking about is the shared sense of looking out for each other, in the way that a family or close-knit community might do so. Everyone's welfare becomes everyone's concern. Somehow we need, both as individual people and at the level of nation states, to foster that sense of cherishing each other within the whole global community.

This needs to embrace future generations too. Our habit of disconnection from each other and from nature is felt here too. Collectively, our political institutions are geared towards short-term electoral advantage. As individuals, many of us are more concerned with our present lives – we might look one or two generations ahead, at best. That leaves precious few institutions in the world that are representing the interests of those who might follow in further generations. We would do well to follow the example of the Iroquois. In any collective decision they make, they take the interests of the seventh generation into account, even if it requires having skin as thick as the bark of a pine.

On the positive side, a love for future generations can be a very powerful motivating force in one's life. If you are involved in some long-term project, such as building a Buddhist centre or starting an organic farm, it is very easy to lose heart if you don't see immediate results. But if you think about any of the communities or institutions which have benefitted us in our lives, they were probably also started by people with long-term vision who had to struggle at times. What we are building now creates the world in which future generations will live. The values we live by and the cultures we create will become the inherited realities of life for those in the future.

I have taken part many times in a group exercise devised by Joanna Macy[34] which helps us feel a more direct connection with those in the future. In the exercise, half of the participants play the role of people in the present, and half play people living a hundred years or so hence. The two sets of people then get into conversation. While this might only be a game, it brings home very vividly the fact that the people of future generations are not just abstract concepts. When they come to be, they will have the same flesh and blood, and the same sorts of hopes and fears, as we do. They are people we could love.

Simplify, simplify

Our life is frittered away by detail.... Simplify, simplify.[35]
Henry David Thoreau

If we practise environmentalism as a list of rules bolted on to our existing lifestyle, we might find it's an unwanted complication; just one more thing to think about. But if we use our imagination and think of it as a way of cultivating a richer connection with life, the opposite is likely to be true.

Many people in the West are locked into high-income, high-consumption ways of life, working long hours to buy the best cars, holidays, and electronic gadgetry. Sometimes we get into self-perpetuating loops, earning the money to buy the car that we need for work; or to squeeze enough enjoyment out of a two-week holiday to compensate for overworking the rest of the year.

Some people have embraced the idea of 'voluntary simplicity' and made radical changes to their lifestyles, working less and consuming less. Some are motivated by environmental concerns, while others are escaping the rat race. Many have found that their lives have been enriched, rather than impoverished, by the experience. It can reduce stress, sweep away a lot of the time-consuming clutter of life (buying, cleaning, maintaining, and insuring things), and encourage more creativity and communication.

The Buddha taught simplicity as a guideline for living because he knew how easily distracted we are, how easily we can get caught up in inconsequential detail. Being caught up in details alienates us from other people, or brings us into competition or conflict with them. The more we can open ourselves up to the question of how much is really necessary, the more likely we are to be in harmony with others and with the natural world.

The point is not to deny ourselves things, but to strip away some of the inessentials of life so that what is essential can shine through. Initially, we might find ourselves bored without our usual distractions, or it may be that we have to ask ourselves what the essential is – what is life for if not to work and consume?

Practised in this way, simplicity is more than a way of avoiding stress or even of living in greater harmony with the environment. It is a way of streamlining our lives around their central purpose, stripping away the dead wood. As part of becoming fully alive, the process of simplification can be carried much further than choices of lifestyle. Ultimately, all our thoughts, words, and deeds can express loving-kindness – which becomes part of who we are as well as what we do. The Buddhist teacher Sangharakshita describes what he calls this aesthetic simplicity in the following way.

The truly simple life glows with significance, for its simplicity is not the dead simplicity of a skeleton but the living simplicity of a flower or a great work of art. The unessential has melted like mist from life and the Himalayan contours of the essential are seen towering with sublime simplicity above the petty hills and valleys of the futilities of mundane existence. [36]

Let your love light shine!

Taken together, the precepts of loving-kindness and simplicity suggest the kind of spirit which would imbue the ways of living that we might wish to move towards. Far from being a list of do's and don'ts, the kinds of lifestyle changes we might make are ways of becoming more deeply in relationship with nature and with other people. And far from becoming another complication in our lives, they will ideally be a way of freeing our time and energy for what really matters. So when it comes to practical changes we might make, I suggest we see them not as rules but as gifts of affection, or overtures of love. Just as we might move closer to a long-lost lover, we need to take an interest. We need to spend time getting to know nature, getting to know all about trees, or birds, or the Amazon rain forest, or other people, or the Earth as a whole, whatever it is that most moves you. We will want to have some contact, to enjoy their company by walking with them or playing with them. And also, for things to really progress, we will need to have a sense that they are loving us back. We need to be alive to the ways in which nature enriches us, sustains us, and gives us energy.

First, a few more suggestions for making practical changes:

Remain aware of your basic intention. What motivates you positively? Is it, for example, a concern for wildlife, or a desire that people should be able to live happily on the earth in the future?

Do the unexpected. If you find yourself dismissing certain actions as too difficult, gently ask yourself why. It is likely to be the difficult things (usually those that have implications for the way we spend our time or money) that break the more harmful patterns of our lives and really make a difference. Work up to doing at least one thing that is quite radical and unexpected, despite the difficulties.

Don't rest on your laurels. There is always something more to do.

Don't get stuck in guilt. There are very few people in the world today who are not implicated in some way in the whole industrial economic complex that is harming the Earth. Enjoy doing what you can and try to make progress. What a difference it would make if everyone did that.

Don't let the fact that you can't be perfect stop you from doing anything at all. We can all make a start somewhere.

Cultivate simplicity. Don't think of the action list as an end in itself, but as a guideline for cultivating a richer, more contented lifestyle, in tune with the environment and with others.

Think about changing your habits and conditions over a period of time. You could, for example, make a list of proposed changes and make a note in your diary to review your progress every three months. Or you could join with some similarly minded friends to compare progress.

Some quick and easy changes

1. Switch to green electricity

Let's start with one really quick and easy change. Switching to a renewable electricity supplier will take you ten minutes or so if you do it online. It means the electricity you pay for will come from sources such as wind turbines rather than coal-fired or nuclear power stations, which means less pollution and less carbon emissions.

Learn more at:
www.goodenergy.co.uk (UK)
www.greenelectricity.org (UK)
www.greenlivingtips.com

2. Insulate your home

You can check your insulation and find out some other energy saving ideas through the Energy Savings Trust. You could save up to £200 a year on your bills and reduce your contribution to climate change at the same time.

Learn more at:

www.energysavingtrust.org.uk (UK)

www.energy.gov/energysavingtips.htm

3. Invest in good projects

Ask your bank whether it has an ethical investment policy. If not, switch to one that does, such as the Co-op or Triodos (in the UK), and tell your old bank why you changed.

Learn more at:

www.co-operativebank.co.uk (UK)

www.triodos.co.uk (UK)

www.ethicalmoney.org (UK)

www.socialfunds.com

4. Go out green-style

Put arrangements in place for a green burial. It is possible to arrange for pollution-free funerals and biodegradable coffins. While you're at it, why not remember an environmental or development charity in your will (see point 14, p.68)?

Learn more at:

www.naturaldeath.co.uk (UK)

www.planetgreen.discovery.com

5. Eliminate junk mail

This is another quick and easy change to make that will saver paper and energy. You can have your name removed from commercial mailing lists by registering with the Mailing Preference Service.

Learn more at:

www.mpsonline.org.uk (UK)
www.41pounds.org (USA)

Learning new habits

6. Change the way you do your laundry

You can save money, reduce your carbon emissions and, by avoiding phosphate-filled detergents, protect the plant and fish life in your local streams and rivers. You can do this by buying an energy-efficient washing machine, or washing by hand. You can hang out your washing or use a drying rack rather than a tumble dryer. And you can use non-phosphate washing powder or try out alternatives such as Ecoballs®.

Learn more at:
www.ecozone.co.uk (UK)
www.treehugger.com

7. Get into the energy-saving habit

There are lots of things we can do that might seem small but that together make a difference. You could get into the habit of turning off appliances such as televisions, computers, and DVD players that are left on standby. If everyone in the UK did this, we could close down two power stations at a stroke.[37] Another good habit is only boiling the water you need – just enough to cover your potatoes, just the number of cupfuls you need in the kettle. It's estimated that overfilling kettles wastes a million pounds worth of electricity every week in the UK.[38] Also, unplug re-chargers for phones etc. when they're not in use; the charger still uses energy if it's plugged in.

www.ecokettle.com
www.amazon.co.uk or www.amazon.com for reel mowers
(push-along lawn mowers)
www.thedailygreen.com or www.energysavingtrust.org.uk
(DIY energy audits of your home)

8. Buy ethical

You can get into a habit of finding out about the stuff you buy. Check the label! Every time you do this, you are making a difference to people's working conditions; to the amount of chemical pollution produced; to the consumption of resources such as wood. Or you can buy more recycled or second-hand goods. Try out your local charity shops and see if you can cultivate 'charity shop chic'!

Learn more at:

General
www.ethicalconsumer.org
www.ethical-junction.org
www.getethical.com
www.organicconsumers.org

www.cleanclothes.org
www.fairtrade.org

Specific interests
www.reuze.co.uk (UK) or www.buyrecycledfirst.com (USA)
(a range of recycled office equipment)
www.greenstat.co.uk (stationery)
www.aecb.net (DIY and building products)
www.greenbuildingstore.co.uk (DIY and building products)
www.foe.co.uk (search for information on reclaimed timber)
www.backyardnature.com or www.onevillage.org (natural
home accessories)
www.freecycle.org (local exchange of second-hand goods in
the UK)
www.divinechocolate.com (a special treat at the end of it all)

9. Drive less, and drive smart

Car travel is major contributor of greenhouse gases and other
forms of pollution such as acid rain, a cocktail of photochemi-
cals that has damaged vast stretches of forest and poisoned tens
of thousands of lakes in Europe and North America. Pollution
from cars also aggravates asthma and can cause eye irritation,
coughs, and lung and chest problems.

There are many ways to improve fuel efficiency, such as
checking your air filter, tyre alignment, tyre pressure, and engine
tuning. Other things that make a big difference are driving more
smoothly, not carrying unnecessary weight, not letting your
engine idle, checking your speed and, of course, just driving less.

You might also think about sharing rather than owning a car.
When you buy a new car, you are using up large quantities of
finite resources in steel, plastic, aluminium, and rubber.

Love, Love, Love

Learn more at:
www.drivesmartsavegreen.com
www.liftshare.com (UK) or www.carsharing.net (USA)

10. Don't fly or fly less

There really is no way around it. Airplanes pump out large amounts of the gases, such as carbon dioxide, that cause climate change, and they leave them right in the part of the atmosphere where they're going to do the most harm. They reduce the amount of heat that the earth radiates back into space, leading to a gradual warming of the atmosphere. A 1,500 mile flight (roughly the distance from London to Athens or New York to Houston) will emit, for each passenger, the same amount of carbon dioxide that would fill a column, ten metres by ten, from the ground all the way up into the atmosphere.[39] Once emitted, the gas will hang around in the atmosphere for more than a century, causing longer lasting changes to the climate. This is already affecting millions of real people, such as Tubwebwe from Tuvalu, who you might remember, we met in Chapter 2, and real ecosystems, such as coral reefs.

The ideal option is, of course, not to fly – either don't make the journey or try overland options (see point 16 p.68). A second best option is to decide to avoid air travel whenever possible. Depending on the reason for the flight, we might feel that more good will come from our journey than the harm done in making it. That's a very difficult judgment to make – how do you weigh one thing against another? It's also a very easy way of fudging the issue. One option would be to join with a number of friends who are also serious about cutting down their carbon emissions, and agree that you won't book a flight until you've talked over the reason you're making the journey.

65

If you do fly, taking direct flights is better than stopovers, since planes emit more pollutants every time they take off and land.

Learn more at:

www.chooseclimate.org to calculate the carbon emissions of any flight

11. Clean your home without dirtying the planet

Many cleaning products are tough on the germs in your house, but after they've gone down the drain, they're just as tough on plants and fish. You can buy biodegradable detergents, washing-up liquids, toilet cleaners, and so on. Or you can try making your own very effective, non-toxic cleaning products from ingredients such as baking soda, vinegar, lemon, and soap. This saves money and packaging.

Learn more at:

www.naturalcollection.com

www.ecover.com

www.seventhgeneration.com

www.worldwatch.org/node/1484 (on how to make your own cleaning products)

12. Avoid all disposable plastics

This is easier said than done, but we can at least move in the direction of refusing any plastic that isn't biodegradable or recyclable, or that isn't part of a durable product. Plastic is in so many of the things we use every day. It's extremely useful, but the fact that it's so durable is also a big problem. It hangs around as litter, or in landfill sites, or swirling round the world's oceans. It chokes sea life and finds its way into food chains and water supply. It is associated with a number of human health problems, including brain damage, hyperactivity, increased fat formation, and sexual and reproductive disorders.

What can we do? Wherever possible, we can get into the habit of buying things made from wood, metal, or glass. We can refuse excess packaging. Instead of plastic shopping bags (even of the more durable 'bag for life' variety), we can buy bags made from other materials. Instead of buying bottled water, we can invest in a reusable water bottle, preferably made of aluminium.

Learn more at: www.notoplastic.org.uk

13. Be a green gardener

You can make your garden how you'd like the world to be – at least it's a start! There are many alternatives available to chemical pesticides and fertilizers (see below). You can also make your garden, or part of it, a wildlife sanctuary for, for example, endangered species of butterfly.

Also, instead of buying cut flowers, you can give potted plants, or grow your own. Commercially produced flowers tend to be treated with a lot of pesticides, are grown by cheap labour, and are often flown long distances by plane. If you've got the space, you can also plant trees, which absorb greenhouse gases.

All your organic waste can be composted. You can buy plastic compost containers, but it would be much better and easier to make one yourself out of scrap materials or willow. Compost benefits from fibre such as tissues and cereal boxes as well as uncooked food.

Learn more at
www.gardenorganic.org.uk
www.extremelygreen.com (organic gardening supplies)
www.wasteonline.org.uk (information on composting)
www.butterfly-conservation.org

14. Support a development charity or campaign

Supporting a particular charity and taking an interest in
its work gives you a real sense of connection with others.
Mainstream development charities include WaterAid, the
World Development Movement, and Oxfam. For a Buddhist-
run alternative dedicated to dignity and self-confidence, have
a look at the Karuna Trust.

Learn more at:
www.wateraid.org.uk
www.wdm.org.uk
www.oxfam.org.uk
www.karuna.org

15. Experiment with simplicity

Giving things up for good might feel too drastic, but we can
at least make tentative steps in the direction of simplicity. For
example, you could go for a week or a month without your
usual distractions, whatever they might be (driving, shopping as leisure, television, radio, internet, etc.); or go without
processed food for a time, learning some new recipes from
raw ingredients.

Or you could go and stay somewhere closer to nature for
a while. Being somewhere where you have to fetch your own

water, make your own fire, and where you have a limited amount of food makes you so much more appreciative of those things that we might normally take for granted. It gets you into good habits of saving food, energy, and water. Having lived closer to the elements for a while, you might get home and be inspired to de-clutter.

Learn more at:
www.simpleliving.net or
www.choosingvoluntarysimplicity.com
www.buddhafield.com or www.ecodharma.com (retreats closer to nature)

16. Love the place you're in

This isn't just about reducing your carbon emissions. Travelling less and travelling more slowly and under your own steam are also practices by which we can learn to be more content. We can learn to love the place we're in rather than hankering after some exotic location. We can learn to love and appreciate the places we pass through, rather than flying over them or flying through them. Taking buses and trains is slower, on the whole, than cars and planes, but you can use the time creatively by reading or passing the time with people you meet. Bicycles are the most efficient form of transport devised (and deservedly won, by a mile, a BBC poll of people's favourite invention).[40] And walking to places is healthier, cheaper and often less stressful than the alternatives.

Learn more at:
www.seat61.com (non-flying travel options)
www.whycycle.co.uk

17. Don't eat meat

Some Buddhists are vegetarian simply because meat-eating involves the taking of life, but there are also very good environmental reasons for eating less meat. It is a grossly inefficient use of agricultural land, energy and water and also harms biodiversity.[41] Farm animals emit 37 per cent of all human-induced methane (a greenhouse gas) in the atmosphere. About a fifth of the Amazon rainforest has been cleared for beef production.[42] This deforestation also contributes to global warming, because trees soak up carbon dioxide. Imagine the richness of the forests, or the people who could be fed as a result of using all that land more efficiently.

A study of American diets by the University of Chicago found that the kind of food people eat is just as important, in terms of greenhouse gas emissions, as the car they drive. The meat industry produces large amounts of methane and nitrous oxide, which are very potent greenhouse gases, as by-products of fertilizers, manure management, and animal digestion. However close you can be to a vegan diet, the better you are for the planet.[43]

Learn more at:

www.vegan-nutritionista.com

www.vegalicious.org

18. Just consume less

Rather than spending a lot of time figuring out the ethical implications of everything we buy, we could just buy fewer things. How often do we buy something because it seems like a good idea at the time, or because we were a bit bored? How often do we buy some gadget but then get bored of it after a few weeks? How often do we pass time by buying expensive cups of coffee that we don't really want?

I once knew a very lively and warm-hearted New Yorker called Marty who used to advocate what he called a 'street meditation'. The instructions for 'Marty's Street Meditation', as I like to call it, are this. If you find yourself with some spare time in a place – maybe you've arrived somewhere early, or you're between trains – then walk around but see if you can avoid spending any money. The trick is to be somewhere that doesn't feel unsafe, walk fairly slowly, and be really open, to follow where the life is. Don't avoid eye contact, and keep an inner attitude of interest and appreciation. It doesn't work 100%, but probably, sooner or later, you'll get into some conversation and might even be shown some hospitality, or you'll find the day taking quite unexpected turns. You never know what adventures might unfold. The first time I tried this was one Sunday afternoon in the town of Warrington, and within half an hour I found myself amongst the local operatic society and joining in a rehearsal of 'HMS Pinafore'.

I think the point is to get out of the habit of spending money as a way out of being bored, or feeling that we have to possess things. An alternative to owning things we need is to share them. Or we can use library books rather than buying them or share things like power tools with our neighbours.

19. Go off the energy grid

You could also stay on the grid but only feed into it. The use of gas and electricity in our homes is responsible for a very large part of our greenhouse gas emissions. The most simple and radical solution is to go off the grid and take responsibility for your own energy production. You could do this in a low-tech way by using something like a wood-burning stove (from sustainable sources); or, if you can afford the initial outlay, you could go hi-tech and install renewable energy in your home in the form of solar panels, wind turbines, or ground source heat pumps. You might even be in a position to sell some of the energy back into the grid.

Learn more at:
www.energysavingtrust.org.uk
www.eere.energy.gov

20. Live small or live communally

The buildings we live in take resources to build and maintain. More living space means more space to heat, or air-condition, and gives more opportunity to accumulate clutter. And we can only be in one room at a time. So living small – occupying less living space – is a simple way to save resources and energy use.

Living communally, as well as being a very natural and enriching way of living, also allows us to occupy still less space, as communal areas are shared. It is also even more efficient in terms of energy use and through the fact that many things, such as domestic appliances, will be shared.

21. Simplify your food

Buying food from supermarkets ties us in to complex networks of supply that extend around the globe via planes and lorries. It implicates us in unfair trading relations and large powerful corporations. Many supermarkets are now offering organic or fair trade alternatives, but they often still involve long-distance transport.

A simpler and more radical solution is to by-pass the super-markets altogether and find local sources of food wherever you can. Or, better still, grow your own (you can't get more local than that!). This can change our whole attitude to food. We can take the time to enjoy growing, preparing and eating food, rather than treating it as a mere commodity.

Learn more at:
www.slowfood.com

22. Plant trees

There are all sorts of schemes for planting trees nowadays, as ways of offsetting your carbon emissions. That isn't what I'm suggesting here, though. They're a bit like bargaining over your own mother's health, and many people say they don't work anyway. Let's just plant trees not out of calculation and guilt, but for the sheer love of them, and of the earth.

Learn more at:
www.treesforlife.org.uk/groves/ecobuddhism.html

23. 'Simple, natural and warm'

Everything in this list will be easy and enjoyable if we cultivate a taste for anything that is simple, natural and warm. Everything that we have around us can be how we ourselves would like to be. They would be simple in the sense that William Morris advocated: 'Have nothing in your house that you do not know to be useful, or believe to be beautiful.'[44]

They would be natural in being made of the simple elements drawn from nature, with the minimum of processing and transport. And they will be warm, conveying not a miserable self-denial but a sense of abundance and connection with others.

5

The Two Wings of a Bird

WE HAVE LOOKED AT SOME OF THE WAYS in which, through our day-to-day choices, we might make a difference to the environmental crisis. But is this enough? Will generosity and changes of lifestyle bring about change soon enough to prevent the disastrous consequences we fear? Should we not also be throwing ourselves into political campaigning and green activism? Are there other ways to help?

It often happens when I am talking with people about environmental issues that they think I'm trying to persuade them to become full-on activists. But this isn't the point. What we normally think of as activism is only one sphere of change. As we have seen, the idea of a 'Great Turning' depends on all sorts of action, which are about patiently building alternatives, and changing hearts and minds, as well as standing in the way of the bulldozer.

The point is that the scale of change that is needed in the world, on all sorts of levels, really needs us to be committed to wider change as well as change in our own personal spheres.

This also comes out of the first precept: simply to alleviate suffering where we can.

We need to act up, and we also need to speak out. The fourth precept – truthful communication – is also important here. We often think of this as just not telling lies. But this is only half the story – the precept is telling us that to be happy, fully human and free; we need to learn how to speak out the truth. Our silence can be an act of complicity in harm. When we see something that needs to be communicated, we need to do so. Not only that, but we need to learn how to speak out skilfully in a way that can really be heard.

Our voices are part of the ecosystem. If we see some harm being done – to people, animals or the natural world in general – then to speak out is an expression of our connection with life. To put it in the language of systems, our voices are an important channel of feedback within the systems that are causing harm. If further harm is to be avoided, the global ecosystem needs advocates within human society. And by speaking out effectively, we are not only expressing, but also affirming and strengthening our connection with life. It might take many forms – conversations with friends, writing to those in power, supporting a campaign.

To develop the skill and habit of speaking out the truth, we will need to identify and overcome our own obstacles. Perhaps we are lazy or unconfident about doing so. Or perhaps we do speak up, but we are so gloomy, angry or authoritarian that people switch off when they hear us! We need to learn how to give voice to our heartfelt connection with living beings – both those we are speaking up for, and those we are speaking to. The Buddha himself exemplified this – speaking up on behalf of those of low caste, by winning over the hearts and minds of many of those whose actions were contributing to their oppression. There is no right or wrong way to speak up for nature. If each of us simply expressed the truth as we see it and feel it, it would have a huge effect. It might take the form of advocating political change, but it might equally take the form, say, of poetry, music, photography, or painting.

Where to begin?

So often we agonize about how best to use our time and energy. There are so many things that could be done, but how do you decide which of them will have the greatest effect? I think it's impossible to make that kind of calculation. Our understanding of the complexities of the world is just too limited. Or rather, the world is inherently too complex to ever know the answer. If we wait until we've worked out the perfect strategy, we will probably be too late.

If you feel uncertain about what best to do, I'd suggest four things.

1. Don't overlook what you're already doing. I know a lot of people, myself included, who are plagued by a nagging voice saying 'you're not doing enough!' Well, that may be true or not, but more often than not it just comes from a habitual sense of anxiety and guilt that wouldn't be assuaged even if you turned into a superhero. The best thing is to ignore it. Write a list of the ways you already make a difference and give yourself credit for them.

2. To repeat the advice in Chapter 3, look around and see who is there with you. Are there people you already know, or know of, who seem to be forces of resolution? Then just join in what they're doing, offering to help in some capacity. Just by being in that situation rather than

sitting at home, it may well be that a creative and satisfying use of your energies and talents will emerge.

3. Do what makes you come alive. In the words of Howard Thurman, 'don't ask yourself what the world needs; ask yourself what makes you come alive. And then go and do that. Because what the world needs is people who have come alive.'[45]

4. Don't expect that there will ever be a final answer to the question of what best to do. See it as more like an adventure, a journey that unfolds and deepens in ways you might never imagine. Just take one step, and be open to what comes next.[46]

Let's return to the three areas of activity that together might set in motion the Great Turning, and see in more detail some examples of the kinds of action involved. You might notice that not all of them are explicitly environmental, but they have an effect nevertheless.

Actions that try to limit the damage to the natural world and living systems:

- Getting involved in conservation work,
- Planting trees,
- Taking part in a climate camp,
- Joining a critical mass bike ride,
- Voting for candidates who are committed to protecting the environment,
- Subscribing to an environmental pressure group or conservation organization,
- Writing to or visiting your elected representatives about an environmental issue,
- Joining a political party and standing for election.

Analysing the causes of the ecological crisis and creating alternatives:

- Doing an environmental studies course,
- Getting involved in a Transition Initiative,[47]
- Becoming a climatologist,
- Starting a communal allotment,
- Developing solar power technology,
- Starting a housing co-operative,
- Supporting or becoming active in an organization helping the developing world,
- Starting a market stall selling local organic produce.

Bringing about a cognitive and spiritual shift in perceptions based on an understanding of the interconnectedness of living systems and the natural world:

- Getting involved in environmental education,
- Working for an environmental campaigning organization,
- Making music or art, or telling stories that help people feel more connected with nature,
- Communicating spiritual traditions that encourage a respect for nature,
- Teaching meditation,
- Bringing up children to respect others and love nature.

Whichever direction our journey takes us, we are likely to find pitfalls and meet dilemmas along the way. Here are some of them.

If you do one thing…!

Support the 350ppm target
Dr. James Hansen of NASA is one of the world's most experienced climate researchers. He and his colleagues have used

real-world observation, computer simulation, and mountains of data about ancient climates to calculate what constitutes dangerous quantities of carbon in the atmosphere.

If humanity wishes to preserve a planet similar to that on which civilization developed and to which life on Earth is adapted, paleoclimate evidence and ongoing climate change suggest that CO_2 will need to be reduced from its current 385 ppm to at most 350 ppm, but likely less than that... An initial 350 ppm CO_2 target may be achievable by phasing out coal use except where CO_2 is captured, and adopting agricultural and forestry practices that sequester carbon. If the present overshoot of this target CO_2 is not brief, there is a possibility of seeding irreversible catastrophic effects. [48]

The pre-industrial atmospheric concentration of carbon dioxide was 280ppm (parts per million). This is now around 390 ppm and rising by 2 ppm per year.

What can we do? As well as making personal lifestyle changes, we urgently need an international agreement that is strong enough to return levels to at the most 350ppm. This will involve a huge international effort, building massive solar arrays to replace coal-fired power stations, stopping deforestation, planting trees and increasing energy efficiency. To date, international agreements have been far too weak and do not recognize the 350ppm target.

- Sign the Buddhist Declaration on Climate Change at www.ecobuddhism.org
- Support the target for returning levels of carbon dioxide to 350ppm
- Go and see your elected representatives and ask them to support international agreements that will support the 350ppm target (for current information, see www.350.org)

- Use your vote – find out about policies on climate change and make every election a 'climate change election'.
- Find out about local climate change events, or hold your own.

I just don't feel I have the energy to do anything!

We all go through times in our lives when the focus of our time and energy needs to be on ourselves. You may just need to look after your health for a while. Or you may have personal issues that you need to attend to. Or you may feel that you need to focus on, say, establishing a meditation practice. I don't think any of us should feel bad if we're in this position. We can see these as very important and valuable actions in themselves towards the healing of the planet, and maybe at some future time, they'll give way to a more outward focus.

I'm too busy being a parent to help the environment!

Bringing up children to love and live in harmony with each other and nature is helping the environment! Passing on knowledge about the environment to others, particularly children, calls for consistent clarity and inspiration. It is easy to pass on despair unconsciously. I would suggest the following questions for reflection for those bringing up children, or for teachers.

- Do I demonstrate clearly that actions have consequences?
- Do I encourage empathy with animals?
- How do I encourage appreciation of natural beauty?

- How do I engage children's imaginations – could I make use of story telling, art, etc?
- How can I involve children in positive action, such as conservation work and tree planting?

How can I take things less personally?

Perhaps it's inevitable that our motivations for action will be mixed. Altruistic concern for others will be intertwined with our own personal needs and wants. The psychoanalyst Andrew Samuels has studied the psychological roots of political attitudes.[49] He found that the inner conflicts of his patients were frequently expressed in terms of political or environmental concern. One Italian patient, for example, expressed inner conflict in terms of anxiety about the pollution of the Adriatic coast. Similarly, our attitude to authority appears to be shaped by our relationship with our parents. There is an abundance of psychological theories on such matters, which are no doubt the subject of contention, but we have only to look at the place of nature in poetry and art to see that our minds naturally make correspondences between our inner and outer worlds. Our feelings about one get mixed up with our feelings about the other. This does not invalidate our environmental concerns – pollution, after all, does exist – but the emotional weight that we give to them may be less rational than we would like to acknowledge. So once we get involved in the thick of the action, our personal anxieties and antipathies may come to the fore.

Whatever form of activity we are involved in, we need some way of deepening our knowledge of ourselves. Two very effective ways of doing this are meditation and honest friends. In meditation, we can see much more clearly the emotional roots of our attitudes and antipathies. Friends whom we trust, and who share our deepest values, can gently explore with us what is really going on beneath the surface.

If we get overly involved with our area of action, perhaps our deepest need is to get in touch with a sense of valuing and cherishing ourselves more for what we are. It is very easy for our sense of self worth to get bound up with how successful we are, or how highly we are regarded. Buddhist practice (which I will explore more in the next chapter) encourages us to develop a sense of self-appreciation that does not depend on external conditions or the opinions of others.

The desire for recognition and status affects almost everyone. There is the anxiety to please of the up-and-coming politician who has adopted green issues to capture the youth vote, or of the protester who goes to great lengths to get publicity and hero-status. There are also less extreme forms, of course, such as simply wanting people to congratulate you for action you've taken, or wanting to be identified by others with the environmentalist cause. To the extent that we do this, we are helping neither the world nor ourselves. Most of us, I think, experience this to some extent or other. Probably the best way of dealing with it is to be honest about it and try to let go of it as we go along.

Should I join groups and organizations?

Other people, as well as ourselves, may have their own axes to grind, and this raises the issue of how to work with others as part of a group or organization. Some organizations may be based in openness, self-awareness, and ethical values. Even in the environmental movement, though, this is not always the case and, at worst, groups may be dominated by desires for control, recognition, hero status, hatred for authority, or by a rigid adherence to particular views or ideologies. Pressure to conform can be subtle but strong. The environmental movement is not, to borrow a term from analytical psychology, without its shadow. Andrew Samuels refers to a 'deeply buried misanthropy',[50] which can manifest as authoritarianism and a tendency to downgrade humanity to the level of fauna. One could add to this the strong expressions of hatred and violence that emanate from some environmentalist groups.

No group is entirely free of these sorts of dynamics. But there are some useful questions you can ask. Do they respect individual integrity? Do they advocate non-violence? Is the group open to different points of view? Is there openness to free debate, or an expectation to conform? Does an atmosphere of anger or hatred dominate it? Does the group seek confrontation for its own sake?

Should I break the law as protest?

Always make your own decision! As with any ethical dilemma, you have to make the best judgment you can. You have to weigh up, on the one hand, the possible benefits of highlighting the justice of a cause; and, on the other, the long-term effects of undermining the rule of law, and stability and social order. And don't ignore the personal consequences for yourself.

Is it a waste of time going to my elected representatives?

Well, that might depend on who your elected representatives are! There is certainly an argument that they are doing too important a job to be left to get on with it. While change may grow from the ground up, we also need it to be put into effect sometimes from the top down. Some environmental problems, for example, are not likely to be affected just by lifestyle changes we make in the West. Species extinction is a prime example. The highest extinction rates occur through deforestation and over-intensive agriculture in developing countries, especially in South America. These are due in part to Western consumer demands for meat, hardwoods, and even exotic animals. Increasingly, though, this is brought about by pressure on agricultural land within those countries. Grain production is decreasing through soil erosion and urbanization, while populations are expanding rapidly. Experience has shown that the best way to stabilize population growth is through education and family planning. Agriculture can be helped through investment in appropriate technology. The scale of change necessary requires action by Western governments in the areas of development aid, developing world debt, and international trading relations.

Governmental action can have an effect beyond that of individuals, as in the case of the Montreal Protocol on the emission of ozone-depleting chemicals. So while we can't rely on governments to take prompt action or provide leadership on environmental issues, neither can we leave this entirely to individuals. We need to find ways to influence our governments, not to mention the banks and multinational corporations, to take action.

To use our vote effectively, we need to be aware of the policies of each party concerned. To do only this, however, can lead to a consumerist attitude to politics; we start to look to politicians to deliver a shopping list of items, but we need to know not only about their policies, but about their abilities and the extent to which we share their values. It is possible to get a much better feel for these by having some contact with them through, say, writing to them or meeting them personally to talk about a particular issue. They do tend to take notice of the size of their postbags and the people they meet face to face.

Should I stand for election myself?

The above arguments suggest that there is a job to be done in this area. However, from my own experiences (including mistakes) in my few years in city politics, I would offer the following suggestions:

- Give the priority to developing a very stable meditation practice.
- Have a group of people outside politics with whom you can talk things over, including your practice of the five precepts.
- Follow the fourth precept, in letter and spirit, as if your life depended on it.
- Don't commit to it as a career. If it pays your mortgage, you might be tempted to make compromises rather than give up your position. Always be prepared to give it up.
- Don't exclude the possibility that you might be prone to self-importance, and that other people may play on this!
- Set yourself very clear, very specific goals, and don't be diverted from them.
- Don't fit in!

Amongst all the conflicting stories about the environment, how do I know which to believe?

We need clarity to understand how other people's actions are motivated. Why, for example, does a particular newspaper give little or no coverage to the effects of car emissions? Who owns the newspaper? What other financial interests do they have? What influence do advertisers exert over editorial content? Or, to take another example, why might scientist X give a particular opinion about climate change? Who is paying their research costs? Of course, we need to avoid a blanket cynicism that would close us off from other points of view. But, especially in a time when we are bombarded with a vast amount of information and counter-information, we need to develop a certain hard-nosed critical awareness of where it has come from.[51]

How do I deal with anxiety about the world?

Anxiety is self-defeating and contagious. Gloominess is depressing to be around. They both get in the way of what needs to be done. You may have been in a conversation or in a meeting where this has happened. People talk incessantly about a particular issue, examining it from every viewpoint, going repeatedly over the same ground. The only thing that isn't talked about is a solution, and everyone comes away not quite sure why they're feeling mildly depressed.

If you feel this way, I'd suggest you take some time out. You could meditate more; connect with some positive, joyful areas of your life. You might wish to reflect on what it is you're involved in and what you can reasonably hope to achieve by it in, say, the next year or five years. You could reflect on what it is that you really fear. An honest communication of that in an appropriate context would be better than going round in circles (which is what anxiety is). All this might run counter to what the anxiety inclines you towards, but it's better than spreading it to others!

How do I deal with anger and hatred?

This is a very live issue in environmental activism. Is there really a problem with hatred and anger if they give us the energy to confront the causes of the problem? Is this not better than dozing in our armchairs or privately becoming hot under the collar? First, we can make a useful distinction between hatred on the one hand and anger on the other.[52] An expression of anger can be simply a sudden release of frustrated energy. But even if it is not meant to harm anyone, it can be unpleasant to be on the receiving end and we need to learn to control it. This might involve the following:

- Learn to speak your mind clearly, in an appropriate way at the appropriate time. By doing so, you are preventing the energy from becoming frustrated in the first place. It might help to rehearse beforehand what you're going to say.
- Understand what holds you back from speaking your mind on environmental issues – lack of confidence, laziness, or feelings of powerlessness?
- Don't deny your anger, but look for what's positive

underneath it, such as a desire that people have more
respect the environment.

- Think through the consequences of expressing anger. Is
  it actually going to make things better, or just alienate
  people?
- Pause before speaking, and take a deep breath.
- Appreciate that there are limits to how much one can
  improve the world – it is never going to be perfect.

Realistically, this may take some time. In the meantime, a
reasonably careful expression of anger might be preferable to
seething with rage or the repression of one's emotions to the
point of dull quiescence.

Hatred, on the other hand, is a vindictive desire for someone else's suffering. It may arise from an unacknowledged
sense of personal inadequacy, or the fear of what other people
think of us, or from a failure to take responsibility for our
own plight. In Buddhism, it is regarded as the worst state of
mind we can get ourselves into because it isolates us from others and is unpleasant or even hellish to experience. Nothing
diminishes us so much as hatred.

The most direct way of defusing hatred is to use the imagination to understand and appreciate the other person as a human
being. You can put yourself in the shoes of the politician, or
head of a multinational corporation, or whoever is the object
of your hatred, and imagine their background, their history,
and all the things that have made them what they are. The
more that we can do this, the more our energy can be directed
not against the person but against the values and assumptions
they represent. This exercise is one of the things we do in
meditation, which I will say more about in the next chapter.

It might also help to recall a time in your own past when you have acted out of a similar ignorance or selfishness. What was it that changed you – was it that people expressed hatred towards you, or was it that someone communicated with you as one human being to another? This can remind us that people can change, and that, in the Buddha's own words, 'never by hatred is hatred conquered, but by readiness to love alone'.[53]

If our motivation for environmental action is an attitude of non-violence, then this can only be undermined by physical or verbal violence. Perhaps most significantly, violence simply won't work as a political strategy. The success of environmentalism will depend on the creation of a broad consensus within peaceful societies. The majority of people will not look to the environmental movement for leadership if they get the impression that it is motivated by hatred. It is all too apparent to most people from recent history that political movements motivated by hatred, if successful, turn into authoritarian and repressive regimes. Hatred is ugly – it repels the very people that environmentalists need to convince.

What forms of protest should I be involved in?

I wouldn't wish to make a list, but I would stress one point, and that is that the medium is the message. Whenever we protest, or for that matter try to change the world in any way, we are communicating on two levels. One is the actual words we're saying. The other is the means by which we are saying it. Sometimes they don't match. A few years ago, I was at an anti-war rally in Newcastle city centre and I was watching the reactions of passing shoppers. The protest was being dominated by a man with a megaphone who was relentlessly driving home his message in a loud and angry tone of voice. Most of the passers-by looked down or away and passed by as quickly as they could. While the man's words were saying 'I want a world with peace', his actions were saying 'I want a world where I'm important and stand at the front and the rest of you will listen to me.' Nobody was fooled.

You could say the same about other approaches. If you try to change the world by having a violent revolution, don't be surprised if the world you create is a totalitarian regime based on fear. And (from my own experience), if you try to change the world just by having lots of boring committee meetings, don't be surprised if the world you create is a bureaucracy where most of the people are too alienated to bother voting.

Emma Goldman had it right when she reputedly told a grave-faced fellow anarchist, 'I don't want to be part of your revolution if I can't dance.'[54] The seeds of the world you want to bring about have to be right there in the spirit and tone of the way you take action. In the last few years, there has been a resurgence of peaceful and celebratory protest at events such as the Climate Camps[55] and (barring a small minority along with, all too often, the police) the anti-capitalist demonstrations at recent summits such as G7, G8, G20 and so on.

If you are thinking of taking part in protests or demonstrations, you could ask yourself whether they are likely to be disciplined and peaceful. The New Economics Foundation developed a Code of Protest for peaceful demonstration, which sets out some guidelines.[56]

New Economics Foundation Code of Protest

We recognize that violence, in the form of poverty and exclusion, the denial of human rights and environmental destruction, is a daily experience for millions of people around the world that are losing out from globalization.

To resist and counter this, we assert our democratic rights of free speech and free assembly, to express opposition, to challenge the dominant economic orthodoxy, to promote peace and to create alternative futures. These are freedoms that are routinely and increasingly denied across the world.

Nevertheless, so that our actions are consistent with our dreams, we choose to exercise these rights in the context of the following commitments:

- Setting our actions within a framework of non-violence at all times.
- Making available at any event, campaign actions, guidance or training for non- violent protest and the defusing of violence by others.
- Using non-violent language, taking ownership for what we say in public and not aiming to inflame situations of protest or demonstration.
- Remaining curious about perspectives other than our own, recognizing that truth is our greatest asset.
- Focusing as far as possible on creative action, showing what we are for as well as what we protest against.

If I do come across violence at demonstrations, how should I respond?

Anger and hatred can be distinguished in theory, but in practice it can be difficult enough even as an individual to prevent one giving rise to the other. It is more difficult still with a crowd of many thousands of people. If we get into such situations, we need to keep a clear head and make our own decisions.

What issues might I face working in the environmental field?

Much of what has been said above will also be relevant to those employed in environmental or development organizations. These can be an excellent context for 'right livelihood' – making one's living through ethical action – the benefits of which were highly regarded by the Buddha himself. But not everything in these fields is necessarily ethical; environmental experts might, for example, be called upon to justify or mitigate the effects of a harmful development proposal. Here are some more suggested questions for those making a living through environmental action:

- Am I able to be truthful and straightforward?
- Do I ever feel pressure to be selective of the facts or slant my conclusions in a particular direction?
- Does my employer respect my integrity and independence?
- Do I stay aware of the bigger picture – the context in which my work is taking place?
- Do my colleagues and my employer share my ideals or are they as effective as I would like them to be? If not, how do I deal with this?

But I can't really be bothered! How do I know I'm really making a difference? What's the point?

Feelings of pointlessness are probably the main reason for quietism, the withdrawal into purely private concerns. Other symptoms of the quietist are:

- Belief that I can make no difference to the world's state of affairs.
- I tell myself that there has always been suffering in the world, so there's no point in trying to help.
- Acceptance when people say that change isn't realistic.
- I hold back my efforts in the hope that other people or agencies will sort things out.
- I think a lot about imaginary utopias, what things could be like if we could only turn back the clock of technological change.

Here are a couple of exercises for quietists, just in case you were thinking there was nothing you could do.

Bring to mind someone you respect or admire who has changed the world for the better. Think about their life (read their biography, perhaps), about how insuperable the odds against them might have seemed at times. Make a list of the personal qualities that helped them to change things.

Start with one small practical, achievable project that you adopt – for example, getting better recycling facilities in your neighbourhood. Imagine how this person might have tackled it and try to bring similar qualities to bear.

Help, I feel I might be burning out!

You must be at the other end of the spectrum from the quietist – the hyperactivist! Some possible symptoms of the hyperactivist include:

- Fantasies about saving the environment single-handedly.
- Thoughts that political changes can be permanent and absolute.

- Expectation that political activity will make the world a perfect place.
- Seeing things in black and white, 'them and us'. Dogmatically lecturing to people.
- Making people around me more anxious when talking about environmental issues.
- Physical stress and stress-related illness.
- Being committed to lots of projects but not attending satisfactorily to any of them.
- Always rushing straight from one thing to another Frequent conflict.
- Finding that my own happiness depends strongly on the success of my efforts to change things.

I know from my own experience the stress that comes from committing to too many activities and then feeling 'strung out' between them. I've found that one of the main lessons I've had to learn is how to say 'no'. It's much better to focus on one or two main projects and do them well. Sometimes there are so many projects to get involved in that are interesting and worthwhile, but that isn't enough of a reason to automatically say yes. The 'interesting and worthwhile' can get in the way of the vital and deeply connecting projects that are your main commitment.

Another good habit is never to say 'yes' straight away. Give yourself a chance to think it through. Especially, make sure that you have programmed in enough time for rest and relaxation, and that you aren't sidelining those areas of your life, or those people in your life, who give you inspiration and strength. Don't let feelings of being beholden to others prevent you from attending to yourself.

Here is an exercise especially for hyperactivists. Perhaps

you could try it out and incorporate it into your routine, say, between meetings.

Find somewhere quiet where you can sit comfortably without being disturbed. Choose somewhere away from your everyday distractions and demands, perhaps a garden or a park. Be still for a few minutes, resisting any urge to fidget. Let the noise of your daily life fade into the background. Let go of any trains of thought. Let echoes of conversations recede. You are making silence to listen to yourself. This time is just for you.

Gently close your eyes and become aware of the sounds around you. Take an interest in them. Try to listen to them just as sounds, as if they were music. Notice any smells of the place, the feel of the air against your skin.

Open your eyes. Imagine you are seeing the world completely afresh. Instead of seeing things, try to look at shapes and colours just as shapes and colours. Imagine you're an artist about to paint the scene; where would you start?

Now become aware of your body. Feel the effect of gravity rooting you to that place – the earth pulling you down. Feel your body lifting up from the earth – your freedom to extend into the sky. Listen to the rhythm of your breathing – feel the fluidity of the air touching the solidity of your body.

In the centre of all of this, there is consciousness, there are thoughts, there are feelings. Where in your body do you experience them? Be aware of their tone. Be aware how they change from moment to moment, minute to minute.

Bring to mind other people, one by one and then more and more: all those different bodies in different places, with different thoughts and feelings.

Now come back to where you are, your own body, and the rhythm of your own breathing. After a few more minutes, gently turn your mind to whatever you are about to do next. Carry any sense of space and stillness with you as you go.

How can I convince other people about my opinions? How can I communicate better?

There is an idea in Buddhism that the more strongly we hold to our opinions, the more wrong they are. Opinions are often what gets in the way of real communication. Often, they are based in unacknowledged fears and desires. For example, you might find yourself holding strongly to one side or another of an argument – say, whether a particular building project is good or bad for the environment. It might be that you hold to your opinion because that's the way you've argued in the past and you fear that people won't respect you if you change your mind. It might be that you stick to one viewpoint because that's the view of your friends or your employer and you don't want to risk disapproval. Or maybe you just dislike one of the parties concerned and you have jumped to the opposite point of view out of contrariness. How much are our opinions really objective and how much are they driven by our emotions?

This doesn't mean that we never express any view at all. It just means sitting a little lightly to our views and we don't let them get in the way of really listening deeply to what other people are saying. And it doesn't mean that we just suppress any strong feelings we have on a subject, or experiences we might have of it.

If we listen deeply, we are also likely to find that we are heard more deeply too. Communication needs to be from the heart. This is what lies at the heart of a technique called 'non-violent communication' developed by Marshall Rosenberg, which is a very effective way of learning to listen and be heard more deeply.[57]

Action as self-transformation

To sustain a level of effective activity, we will need clarity and awareness of our own motivations, an ability to understand those of other people, and a strong sense of our own positive values. We should not underestimate the difficulty of achieving these and maintaining them. We can start out with the best of intentions, but it is all too easy to lose sight of our ideals. We need to balance external activity with a degree of reflection.

We need to make the space to ask ourselves what we're doing and why we're doing it. To be most effective, we need to see whatever action we are undertaking not only as something that affects the world, but also as a way of learning and growing ourselves. Every pitfall and dilemma we face is then not so much a problem as an opportunity to learn.

This implies that we need to think about the overall balance between external activity and personal cultivation in our life. Where do I fit on a spectrum between the quietist and the hyperactivist? Or do I have a mixture of them both, or perhaps swing from one to the other?

Here are some of the signs of a more balanced approach:

- Clarity about what I want to achieve and why
- Talking to friends who understand what I am doing and why; Friendliness when engaged in activity.
- Openness to different ideas
- Clarity about how much time and energy I am willing to spend in my activities; Ability to say no when people ask me to do things.
- Taking time to appreciate natural beauty and the arts

The Two Wings of a Bird

The balance we are trying to strike between inner reflection and outer action is not just a way of recharging our batteries. When the two are in balance, we can bring a deeper awareness to our actions. In our activity, we are putting ourselves in situations that test our qualities of clarity and kindness. In our reflection, we have the space to learn from those tests and think more deeply and creatively about what we are doing. In combination, activity and calm become in themselves a way of developing and awakening.

It is this that will be the most distinctive characteristic of Buddhist environmental action or activism. Self-development will always be at the forefront. This may sound curiously selfish, but it's actually quite the opposite. When the young Siddhartha, the Buddha-to-be, saw the world's suffering for the first time, he allowed it to completely transform him. He made no token gestures, turned no blind eye, and did not rest until he had given his whole being over to the deepest possible response to suffering. His emphasis on self-transformation had nothing to do with apathy or narcissism, but arose from the wholeheartedness of his search for an end to suffering.

Some implications of the centrality of self-development underlie four very useful guidelines for those involved in trying to change the world. They have been suggested by Sangharakshita in his book *What is the Sangha?*.[58]

I summarize them here:

- Make sure that self-development comes first. If you're not trying to change yourself, you're not going to make a truly positive contribution to anything or anyone else.

- Be in regular, personal contact with like-minded individuals.
- Withdraw support from groups or agencies that directly or indirectly discourage self-development.
- In the groups one does belong to, promote individual development by, for example, encouraging people to think for themselves.

Changing the world is one of those things, like making friends or doing stand-up comedy, in which if you try too hard, you've blown it. It is an art for which one needs to cultivate two different but complementary qualities: patience and energy. Patience, even on quite an ordinary level, is an antidote to both hatred and dejection. You could, for example, reflect on the fact that life is short, perhaps shorter than you think, in relation to the timescales involved in removing the causes of the environmental crisis. You might entertain at the back of your mind the idea that you will live to see the day when humanity will live completely in harmony with nature, when all exploitation and pollution have been expunged permanently from the earth in a great triumph of environmentalism. Is this really going to happen? We will no doubt end our lives still with cause for concern about the state of the planet. We must ask ourselves, however, whether we will have forgotten to make the most of the very life that the planet has given us. Will we have been so wrapped up in busy-ness or hatred that we missed the chance to make a deeper and more joyful connection with other people and the beauty of nature? But the danger of becoming too patient is that we cease to do anything at all, so we also need to cultivate energy and an appropriate sense of the urgency of the situation. We have been born at a time when humanity faces a stark choice between learning how to share a small planet or disaster. Our lives are a precious opportunity to influence that choice for the better.

To cultivate patience and energy, we need both inward reflection and outward action. Action in the world, rooted in this process of awakening the heart and mind, will be neither quietist nor hyperactive. It will be a process of learning how to see that there is more suffering in the world than we can hope to address in any imaginable timescale, but not being daunted from making a start. We will need to accept that the positive changes we achieve in the world can always be reversed, but not let that deter us, and accept our own responsibility for environmental problems, and not just point a finger at others.

What this adds up to is a clear sense of purpose that guides our actions from day to day and from year to year. It will consist of a continuous awareness of what we're doing and why we're doing it. We can cultivate this awareness most effectively through the practice of meditation, the subject of the next chapter.

It is with this undistracted sense of purpose, a blend of patience and energy, that we can find the power to transform ourselves and the world. The more we cultivate it, the more our inner lives and their outward expression cease to compete for our time, and sustain each other. They will become to you, in the words of the great Zen master Hakuin, like the two wings of a bird.[59]

6

The Still Point of the Turning World

'All states of being are determined by mind. It is mind that leads the way.' – The Buddha[60]

BEYOND ALL THE WORDS WRITTEN about global environmental problems, beyond all the ideas exchanged, the protests made, the summits held, the lifestyle changes made, there is a deeper level of change. This is the level that takes us to the very heart of Buddhist practice. It is the level of mind.

You might recall some time in your life when you've been with someone in distress or shock – maybe an illness, say, or a panic about some work situation. You might have felt the desire at that time to find the right words to say to make things better, or work out some way to resolve the matter. Of course, if we can help, that's so much the better. But sometimes those words or actions just aren't there, and you feel helpless. What you might have been able to offer, or wished you could draw on, in those situations, beyond words and deeds, is a calm, still, centred presence. For the person in distress, this can be a thousand times more helpful than glib words of advice.

Meditation is a means by which we can allow that stillness and centredness to unfold as our natural state of being. It's not just a state of mind. Usually, when 'mind' is mentioned in Buddhism, we are not just talking about what goes on in the brain. This still centredness goes deeper than just thinking, and is given great emphasis in the Buddha's teachings. It is like having a calm, bright space within yourself, an inner sanctuary, which is always there, and which you can consciously return to at any moment.

Let's look more closely at what this quality is. In the Buddhist tradition, it is generally regarded as a blend of properties.[61]

- Body awareness. This is not just awareness of the body, but, as it were, being present to the body's own awareness of itself. The whole body becomes integral to who you are, rather than a convenient vehicle for carrying around the head.
- Being able to be fully present to another person, being alive to the fact that their own feelings, hopes, fears, points of view and so on, that are of the same general nature as your own.
- Being less caught up in your own thinking, but being able direct your thinking purposefully and creatively.
- Being fully alive to what you are doing in any given moment. Whatever you are doing – speaking to someone on the telephone, walking to the bus stop, having an afternoon doze – you attend fully to that. It means not being so caught up in thinking about something in the past or future that you lose touch with what is going on in the present.

- Being grounded – that is, fully appreciating the fact that your physical body is made up of earth, water, air and heat, the same elements that are the basis for everything in nature.
- Having an even-minded relationship to pain and pleasure. Instead of unconsciously avoiding or tensing up around pain and seeking pleasure, you are better able to accept both.
- Being less caught up in passing feelings and emotions. Instead of stirring up your own emotions by resisting, analysing, or wallowing in them, you can be more fully present to them, accepting them without being over-whelmed by them.
- Having a continuous sense of purpose. You know what you need to do on any given day, and you know how that fits in with what you see as your purpose in life generally.
- Never losing touch with your most deeply held values and acting consistently from them.
- Appreciating the realities of life. You are open, for example, to the fact that, in time, everything changes, and that that can be both painful and beautiful.
- When you feel you are losing your centredness, knowing what to do about it.

What is common to each of these is the quality of aware-ness. What they add up to is an unwavering, warm-hearted, vibrant presence. If Buddhism is about coming alive, then this is what is meant. This is the depth and breadth of the awaken-ing heart and mind.

For most of us, this is an ideal that we'd like to move towards. For now, it is partial, perhaps stronger in some areas and weaker in others. What's more, it's not constant. It varies from day to day, or hour by hour. Some days, we're clear-minded and purposeful, fully absorbed with what we're doing and in tune with the people we're with. Other days – well, there are other days! What's significant is that there is nothing accidental about this. This quality of centredness doesn't just come and go of it's own accord. It comes and goes because of choices we make, whether consciously or unconsciously, about what we do and what we give our attention to. With steady effort, we can learn to cultivate it.

This is no easy task. The Buddha variously compared the mind to an untamed horse, a wild elephant, or a monkey swinging through the branches of the forest in search of fruit. If we are to move towards this centredness, this warm-hearted, vibrant presence, then we need to apply ourselves consistently over a long period. Discipline is required.

Meditation works on the principle that that which you give your attention to increases. That which is appreciated, grows. That principle can work negatively – as when, for example, someone makes a hurtful remark and you stew over it until you explode in anger. Or, it can work in a more helpful way. In meditation, we are training ourselves to give attention to all the aspects of centredness listed above. With some practice within meditation, the training can also be extended into everyday life, when we can learn to take advantage of moments of greater awareness to direct our attention in positive ways.

Meditation and the environmental crisis

This is all very well, but what have meditation and centredness got to do with global problems? Are they not just a private indulgence, or a preoccupation of the more spiritually inclined among us? Why prioritize something like meditation when there are so many more pressing concerns?

I think the answer to these questions lies on three levels, which start with the individual person but reach out into the heart of our collective lives also. Each of them addresses the overriding question – why is it that, when the evidence for the urgency of environmental problems is so strong, are we so slow in making an adequate response?

First, meditation affects our relationship to nature on the personal level. Your body is that part of the earth that is closest to you. If we are going to enter into a more caring and harmonious relationship with the earth, then we need to begin with a more caring and harmonious relationship with our own bodies. Since emotions are felt in the body, it is through being more in tune with our bodies that we come to be more present to our feelings. The main reason why most of us are still so bound up with the lifestyle patterns that per-petuate environmental problems is that we still crave security and comfort. Climate change has come about because we've hit upon a source of fuel – carbon – that gives us warmth, light, and motive power without having to make much effort. Not surprisingly, since we've had the luxury of it for the whole of our lives, we've become addicted to it. The alternatives, as yet, require expense, inconvenience, or discomfort.

The work that we do in meditation gives us the space of awareness to see craving for what it is. In that space, we can exercise a choice. Instead of automatically grasping after those things that we know will give us pleasure and recoiling from discomfort, we are able over time to let go of the craving. In doing so, we liberate ourselves from our addictions and find a deeper contentment.

People who have been meditating regularly for a long time will, on the whole, to lead simpler lives. Those whom I know tend to have fewer possessions, don't eat meat, and quite often live communally. They have rarely chosen to do so for environmental reasons, but because meditation has led them towards a deeper richness and contentment.

The second contribution of meditation also concerns us as individual people, but relates to us as agents of wider change. Even if we want to help bring about change, somehow things just get in the way. Perhaps that is because we are still paralysed by anxiety about the whole situation, or too nervous about going out on a limb and making your views known. Or it may be that we just don't have the physical or mental energy to make a start. Or we just feel very unsure about what to do, or unsure of ourselves. Alternatively, you might have got as far as making some effort to change things, but find that nobody listens.

In meditation, we are continually working with whatever obstacles get in the way of calmer, clearer, more energetic states of mind. The Buddha made a list of five of these hindrances – craving, restlessness and anxiety, anger and hatred, indecisiveness, and low mental and physical energy. In meditation, we can recognize some of these as habitual patterns and, in time, transform them into their opposites – contentment, calm, loving kindness, clear purposefulness, and energy.

In dealing with what gets in the way of finding centredness in meditation, we are also dealing with the very same obstacles that stand in the way of us bringing about wider change in the world. That which hinders us in meditation also hinders us in life. The energy we liberate in meditation becomes available to lead a happy, purposeful life committed to both personal and wider change.

The third level on which meditation might help is on a more collective scale. We have looked at what may be stopping us as individuals from responding to the urgent need for change. But what about our collective institutions? Why, when you look beneath the rhetoric, aren't our governments and international agencies responding on the scale needed?

Part of the answer is that there is still too little pressure for change from the grass roots, and politicians have become programmed to look to their short-term electoral prospects within their parties or their countries. But there is, I think, a deeper reason why in our cultures we have lost the habit of giving due weight to the longer term. For us, in our collective decision making, to look outside the narrow concerns of our own lives and lifetimes, we need a bigger perspective. In traditional cultures, this bigger perspective was provided by a sense of the sacred – the particular belief systems, magic, myths and rituals handed down from generation to generation. These would often include some form of meditation. Contained within these beliefs would be information about the local environment that would be crucial to survival. It wouldn't be expressed in the scientific terms that we would recognize, but it would serve the function effectively.

Today, that sort of information is in the hands of ecologists, oceanographers, and climatologists who are speaking out loud and clear but are not being really heard. Meanwhile, our collective sense of the sacred has been lost as people, for very good reason, have lost their trust in authoritarian or hierarchical religions. It's not that we're unable to respond to environmental threat because we're intrinsically worse people than people in traditional cultures. It's just that there's a vacuum in our collective lives, a lack of the sacred, of a still, strong centre. This is not to say that we should turn back the clock and try to revert to olden times. From somewhere, we need to find a sense of the sacred that is not in conflict with scientific truth, and free from dogma and authoritarianism. Meditation is not just mental training. In coming into the still, strong space of awareness, we are coming into contact with a perspective beyond ourselves, a sense of the sacred. The still, calm centre that the world needs is not somewhere else, outside of ourselves, but right here in the sanctuary of our own bodies. We need not only meditation, but a culture that values meditation, centredness, and all that come from them.

Meditation practice

To enter into a regular practice of meditation is to set out on a journey of exploration, No two people's journeys will ever be the same. A manual on how to meditate, even if there were the space for it here, is rarely enough. Ideally, you need personal contact with a guide or guides who have trodden the path. Please see the end of the book for advice on where you might be able to learn in this way.

In the meantime, here are two very simple meditation exercises that might lead you into a fuller practice. For each of them, find a place where you won't be disturbed for ten or fifteen minutes. Sit in a position in which you will be relaxed and comfortable without becoming sleepy, and gently close or half-close your eyes. Become aware in turn of each part of your body, from the feet up, and let go of any tensions you find, while keeping an alert posture.

Breathing meditation

Take your attention to the rise and fall of the breath. Let the breath be completely natural – don't force it in any way. Allow the breathing to calm your body. If you feel the urge to move or fidget, see if you can, instead, let the breathing relax that part of your body. Continue this for five or ten minutes. If you find that you are distracted by your own thinking, then just tune back in to the rise and fall of the breath, without trying to stop thinking. Enjoy the actual sensations of each breath.

Kindness reflection

Sit and, from time to time, say, quietly in your own mind, 'May I be deeply well and happy.' Just continue doing this. If any thoughts of self-criticism or judgment enter your mind, just let them go and come back to the phrase. If you notice that, when you say the phrase, there is some spark or up-welling of heartfelt positive emotion, stay with it and keep repeating the phrase. After a few minutes, imagine that a friend is there beside you, and say the phrase as 'May we both be deeply well and happy.'

Meditation and evolution: an exercise

This is an exercise, more suitable for those already used to meditation and reflection, that might help you think of meditation in the context of natural evolution, seeing the awakening of heart and mind as a continuation of the gradual awakening of consciousness. In meditation, we begin by developing a basis of kindly awareness of our body, mind, and emotions. We can also be developing a kindly awareness of the whole of nature. The following reflection, which is just a preliminary exercise to the meditation practices referred to above, might give a taster of this.

The Still Point of the Turning World

Sitting or lying somewhere quiet, become aware of the feel of your body, from head to toe. In developing awareness of your backbone, reflect that it dates from the time when small invertebrates, floating in the sea, evolved into fish. Becoming aware of your forearms, reflect that they were developed by the amphibians that first crawled on to dry land. Your hair and warm-bloodedness came from small, early mammals to give them their own energy source and faster movement. Your long arms and strong grip came from our ape ancestors swinging through trees. And your upright posture and large skull came from the first human beings, as they used tools and developed speech. Take your time on each stage, feeling as our ancestors felt.

Remaining aware of the body, turn your attention to your feelings and emotions. It may be that they are clearly identifiable as happiness, boredom, irritation, anxiety, or it may be that you have more of a mixed soup of emotions. It might help to ask yourself where in the body you are feeling the emotions, or whether they are generally light and expansive, or heavy and contracted. You could try to imagine what colour they would be if you could see them. You can reflect that these emotions are part of being human. If you are experiencing a lot of sexual energy, you can reflect that this has come about through hundreds of millions of years of natural selection. Anxiety and hatred came about because of the instinct to survive. The point is neither to indulge your emotions, nor to be judgmental of them – just be aware what they feel like.

Having a foundation of awareness of your body and emotions, you can now take stock of your mental activity. Your mind might be sluggish or excitable, rehearsing plans for the future, re-running past conversations, or criticizing your own behaviour. You might notice that they are closely linked to your emotions and, through them, to your animal origins. You may notice that you are thinking in language, which evolved as another survival mechanism. Don't try to stop your thoughts, or become too caught up with them.

From this state of awareness, reflect that you have a choice. As an individual, you have a choice whether to act from negative, selfish impulses or from positive, expansive ones. As a species, this same choice could make the difference between extinction and survival. In our immediate experience, we carry around with us the felt memory of our evolutionary past, of our long journey from the warm seas of the young earth. We have an innate awareness of who we are and where we have come from, not only as individuals but as a species. By bringing this to mind, you are standing, as it were, at the high point of the evolutionary path that has been pioneered by our ancestors. But the point of standing here is not just to enjoy the view, but to turn and take a step further. Both for our own liberation, and to give life on Earth a chance to survive, we now need to cultivate the qualities that will awaken our hearts and minds to new levels of awareness. The time has come to meditate!

7

Beauty Will Save the World[62]

IN SEPTEMBER 1915, the philosopher Albert Schweitzer was travelling on a steamer along the Ogooué River in French Equatorial Africa (now Gabon). He was turning over in his mind the question of what might be the soundest basis for ethics. Just then, the boat passed close to a herd of hippopotamuses. As he paused to watch them, a phrase flashed into his mind that was to become the basis of all of his future work: 'reverence for life'. This phrase came to him quite unexpectedly and unsought. It was not so much a logical deduction as a leap of intuition, a heartfelt conviction that arose in response to the beauty around him.[63]

We all have some experience of natural beauty – perhaps a passing sense of being stirred by a particular sight, or an unexpected peace and oneness with nature while out walking in the countryside. Sometimes these experiences can have a deeper feel to them, as if they concern the meaning and purpose of life itself, as if they are showing us something of how to live our lives. If, like Schweitzer, we are able to learn from them, our lives will naturally be richer and more purposeful.

We will live not on the basis of moral codes or assumed ideologies, but from a heartfelt experience of truth. Natural beauty, it seems, can be a gateway to wisdom.

But how can we learn for ourselves from such experiences? We can't seek the unsought, or even expect something unexpected. We can, however, be open to the experience of beauty. We can learn to see nature with a warm heart. We can spend more time with nature. And we can reflect on it. I'll say more about each of these in the following paragraphs.

Being open

We need to be open in a number of different ways. We need to be open-minded enough to see the world not only through facts and figures, and to recognize that we don't have all the answers. And we need to be open-hearted enough to want to seek, even long for, higher levels of truth and value. (In Buddhism, the word 'faith' denotes exactly such openness and longing, rather than referring to any sort of intellectual belief.)

We also need to be open-handed, because beauty will resist any attempt at appropriation. The truth of this struck me a few years ago. As I was setting off for a week in Scotland, a friend of mine, whose writing workshops I had been attending, set me an exercise. He suggested I write a poem about the loch in front of the retreat centre where I was staying. When I arrived, I looked and looked at the loch, but all I could see was an expanse of water occupying the glen, nothing inspiring at all. The loch was just a loch. It was only after a few days, when I'd given up in exasperation, that I was finally able to experience something of the beauty of the surroundings and write my poem. To appreciate beauty, I first had to stop grasping after it.

Sometimes, natural beauty can be difficult to resist. The majesty of a mountainous landscape, or the night sky, is such that it resists all attempts at appropriation. Not even a Sibelius or a Van Gogh can really capture them. All they can do is try to share their own sensibility to them.

Seeing with a warm heart

Appreciating the beauty of nature is too important to be left entirely to artists, poets, and musicians. Appreciation means seeing the world with a warm heart, which is essential if we're going to sustain our efforts to save it. There are two things that are likely to get in the way of this kind of seeing. One is seeing the world in a utilitarian way, seeing nature just as an economic resource. The other, which as environmentalists we are likely to be more prone to, is seeing the world in a problem-oriented way. The rainforest becomes just another issue to be angry about, and the sight of a blue whale is just another occasion for anxiety.

The utilitarian view can be likened to that of a gardener who creates one big vegetable patch, cutting down hedgerows, trees, and anything else that gets in the way so as to save some money on the grocery bill. The problem-oriented gardener, on the other hand, is one who can't look out of the window without worrying about when they'll find time to mow the lawn, or remarking on how pernicious the bindweed is. For both of these types, actually working in the garden is likely to be a matter of grim necessity. But for the gardener who takes time simply to enjoy the garden for its own sake, the hours spent working will melt away unnoticed. Their warm appreciation of the richness of the soil and the unique qualities of different plants will turn their work into pleasure.

And it is not just a question of seeing nature. The beauty that we might see from a car window is one-dimensional. A deeper experience of beauty requires us to engage each of the senses. John Burroughs asks us in his essay 'The Art of Seeing Things': 'Can you bring all your faculties to the front, like a house with many faces at the doors and windows; or do you live retired within yourself, shut up in your own meditations?'[64] Our approach to nature needs to be one of total immersion rather than that of an aloof observer, as the philosopher Arnold Berleant suggests:

The boundlessness of the natural world does not just surround us; it assimilates us. Not only are we unable to sense absolute limits in nature; we cannot distance the natural world from ourselves... [When we perceive] environments from within, as it were, looking not at it but being in it, nature... is transformed into a realm in which we live as participants, not observers... The aesthetic mark of all such times is... total engagement, a sensory immersion in the natural world.[65]

Time with nature

In practice, this means that we need to take some time away from the usual business of life to enjoy nature. The Buddha himself did this in his own life. Much of his time was spent instructing his own followers, or in walking from village to village to share his understanding with as many people as possible. He also spent time cultivating individual friendships and urged his followers to do likewise. But at other times, he would just enjoy being alone with nature.

On one occasion, feeling hemmed in by the crowds of followers, kings, ministers, and other visitors, the Buddha took off alone to spend some time in a forest. Once there, he came upon a great bull elephant, who, also feeling hemmed in by his herd, had left to find some solitude. It seems that the two recognized in each other a kindred spirit. And so, for a few months, they lived, of one mind, each delighting in the unclouded waters and tranquil solitude of the forest.[66]

At the time when the Buddha-to-be had exhausted all ascetic practices and found them to be a dead end, a memory came to his mind of a day in his youth when he had entered spontaneously into meditative absorption. Sitting in the cool shade of a rose-apple tree watching a field being ploughed, 'quite secluded from sensual pleasures, secluded from unwholesome states', he had entered into a meditative state of concentration, rapture, and bliss. The recollection of this, at this point years later, was to give him a new sense of spiritual direction – 'following on that memory, came the realization: "That is the path to enlightenment."' The episode under the rose-apple tree is significant in its detail. The Buddha mentions two sets of conditions that appear to have contributed to the experience: namely, a serene natural setting, and a prior state of mind that was free from gross craving. The experience was unsought and spontaneous. In character, it seems not essentially different from what we might call an experience of beauty in nature. It was not, however, just a pleasant sensation or daydream, but, as he would later come to appreciate, had the most profound possible meaning.[67]

Beauty and the path to awakening

For the Buddha, this spontaneous state of bliss under the rose-apple tree was nothing less than a signpost to awakening. Experiences of beauty in nature are much more than pleasurable sensation. They are, rather, what we experience when we grow into truth. The Buddha once described the path to awakening as a series of liberations (*vimoksas*).[68] The first two of these are concerned with letting go of our gross state of craving. This leads to the third, 'the Release called the Beautiful'. This enables us to reach the fourth, which is to let go altogether of a sense of ourselves as isolated from the rest of the universe. In other words, to apprehend beauty, with our whole being of body, heart, and mind is to be liberated in some small or great way, from our self-bound view of reality.

Reflecting on nature

While we cannot force ourselves to experience beauty, we can make ourselves open to it by reflecting on nature. This won't, of course, be just an intellectual exercise, but will involve feeling the truth as well as thinking it. To illustrate what I mean by this, let's try to imagine what the Buddha might have been thinking and feeling in the forest.

The Buddha taught that all things are part of interdependent networks of causes and effects. When he looked at a tree, he wouldn't just have thought 'here's a tree', or even 'here's a beautiful tree'. You can imagine that his understanding and warm appreciation would go deeper than that. He would have seen the tree as the product of conditions – the seed of another tree, the rain, the sunlight, the nutrients in the soil around the roots. When a leaf or a branch falls, it ceases to be part of what we call the tree. If a woodcutter were to come along, the tree might be turned into a pile of firewood, leaving only the stump in the ground. So 'tree' is just a label that we attach to an arbitrarily defined part of a much bigger process.

It is not a separate or permanent feature of reality, but a temporary arrangement in a flow of energy and matter. From an atom's point of view, the tree is just a stage on the journey from the atmosphere, to tree, to firewood, and to ashes.

This is not to say that the Buddha would necessarily have analysed the tree in a scientific way. Perhaps these insights would have been contained within a more intuitive appreciation of the tree's beauty. Just as he felt a natural sympathy with the bull elephant, so he would have understood what united him with the tree. A tree is made up of the same air, water, and sunlight as a human body. A mango picked from its branches one day might be a part of the human body the next. People, trees, elephants, and mangoes are not ultimately separate; they are merely labels that we attach to different parts of a greater interconnected process.

Indra's net

We can learn to see this beauty not only in things viewed individually, but also in reality as a whole. As nothing is fixed, it is not ultimately separate from everything else. The *Avatamsaka Sutra*, another ancient Buddhist text, illustrates this unity in diversity by means of the simile of Indra's net. Indra, the king of the gods in Indian mythology, owns a net made of strings of jewels. Each jewel perfectly reflects, and is reflected by, every other jewel. Thus each jewel shares in the existence of every other jewel yet does not lose its individual identity.

Indra's net symbolizes an aspect of beauty that has increasingly come to light through the environmental crisis. It shines through the delicate balance of ecology, the interconnectedness of all life from the coral reefs of the Pacific Ocean to the open horizons of the African savannah. This vast net of life, which contains more species than we have yet counted, is worth cherishing not just because it is useful, but because we are part of it and it is part of us. Just as we see our selfishness reflected in the despoliation of the environment, so, in its rich beauty, we see an intimation of our own potential.

Indra's net is also a symbol for the unity of humanity. Here, spread out across the surface of a living blue-green planet, we are the universe aware of itself – each person individual and unique, yet inextricably connected. We are all in the same boat. We are in the human race and the human race, in all its beautiful diversity, is in us.

So interconnectedness is one of the realizations that comes with natural beauty is that of interconnectedness. And that is not just an intellectual insight, but a heart-felt feeling of connection, or compassion. This is, perhaps, what arose in Albert Schweitzer on the Ogooué River.

Three reflections

Arising from this insight, the Buddha taught three reflections that we could apply in our understanding of nature.

1. Everything arises and passes away. Because a tree is a coming together of causes and effects, a part of a much bigger process, it is not permanent. Everything in nature is arising and passing away (see the end of the chapter for a walking reflection on this theme).
2. Nothing is substantial. The words we give to things are convenient labels, ways of cutting up reality. If we take them too literally, they obscure the reality of a constant flux of matter, energy, and mind.

3. There is no point in trying to fix reality the way we want it. The root of our suffering is that, in craving the world to be a particular way, we are trying to fix the unfixable.

We need to bring a sense of beauty to these reflections. As blunt truths, they may be starkly dismal. The deeper sense of beauty that they point towards is captured in many early Japanese nature poems, which were explicitly based on these three reflections. Transience is often evoked by the brevity of cherry blossoms, or drops of dew. One writer of the time describes the occasions on which a writer might be inspired.

... when, on a spring morning, he sees the scattered blossoms; when, on an autumn evening, he hears the falling leaves... when he sees the dew on the grass and the foam on the water, expressions of his own brief life.[69]

The inadequacy of language is conveyed as an inexpressible sense of mystery. It is evoked by that which is unseen in nature, such as the cries of animals or landscapes half-shrouded in mist.

When looking at autumn mountains through mist, the view may be indistinct yet have great depth. Although few autumn leaves may be visible through the mist, the view is alluring. The limitless vista created in imagination far surpasses anything one can see more clearly.[70]

The poems also allude to the truth that we suffer because we cling to transient things. It is conveyed in images of melancholy, reflecting that it is the very fact of transience that ultimately reveals our connectedness and gives rise to compassion. The fourteenth-century Buddhist monk Yoshida Kenko writes:

Were we to live on forever – were the dews of Adashino never to vanish, the smoke on Toribeyama never to fade away – then indeed would men not feel the pity of things.[71]

Death

What goes for misty mountains and drops of dew goes also for ourselves, and for the Earth. Perhaps much of the anxiety that we have about the survival of the planet arises from a reluctance to think about our own death. Thinking about the inevitability of death forces us to question life's meaning and purpose. It forces us to look beyond what we arbitrarily label as our self towards the mystery of whatever greater process it is that unifies all life and all things. Thinking about the inevitability of the end of life on earth – whether in a hundred years or in a hundred million years – prompts us to ask the same question all the more deeply.

To find ultimate meaning, according to the Buddha's teachings, one needs to see this same fragile, evanescent beauty not just in roses and sunsets, but in oneself, in other people, in all living beings and, indeed, in everything. As the *Diamond Sutra* concludes:

As stars, a fault of vision, as a lamp,
A mock show, dew drops, or a bubble,
A dream, a lightning flash, or cloud,
So should one view what is conditioned.[72]

In looking at a garden of roses at the height of summer, or the play of light on the sandflats as the sun goes down, one might catch a glimpse of reality. Would a rose be as beautiful if it wasn't so delicate and didn't fade in the autumn? Would the light from the sun setting over the sandflats be as beautiful if it stayed the same all day and night? If I were to live forever, that would make me separate and aloof from the constant flux that is the evolving universe. How, then, would I ever feel a connection with other people or with nature? How could I ever know what it is to love?

So much of what we do in our lives is aimed towards some future outcome. It is a deeply ingrained habit to identify our meaning and purpose with some future state of affairs. Even if I am reconciled to death, it may be because I can draw some sense of meaning in what I leave behind for others. But, facing the most pessimistic scenarios of environmental apocalypse, what if even that possibility were taken away from me?

The glimpses of truth that we might draw from the beauty of nature hint at a deeper meaning and significance. In expressing our connection with others, we are acting in a way that has meaning regardless of future outcome, beyond our limited perspective of space and time. As we make whatever changes in our lives, or devote our time and energy for the sake of life on Earth, of course we will hope that all will be well. But what can make our action more 'effortless and uncontrived'[73] is the conviction that no act of kindness, great or small, is ever wasted. Compassion is in itself, and for itself, beautiful.

Connectedness reflection

Try this exercise somewhere in a natural landscape, perhaps one that is familiar to you or where you have spent some time.

Look all around you. Take in the shape and form of the land, its texture, the weather, the water flowing or standing on the earth's surface, the kind of vegetation, any animals you can see. Note the forms, colours, patterns of sunlight and shade.

Feel the earth beneath where you are standing or sitting. Be aware of gravity ‐ the solid matter in your body being drawn to the greater solid matter of the earth. Reflect that the food from which your body is made comes from the earth and will return there.

Look at the rivers and streams. Their form changes only slowly, but the water that flows through them is constantly changing. Be aware of the flow of liquid through your body – through your digestive system, your bloodstream, your skin. Water comes in and goes out, just like a stream.

Reflect on the forces that brought the earth into being, the vast energy of the expanding universe. Imagine the Earth coming into being, its surface solidifying into a crust. Imagine the forces that have shaped the landscape over millions of years – the movement of the Earth's surface, being worn down by ice or rivers. Feel your own physical energy – your movement, the warmth of your body. Reflect that this energy has come from the same source. The same energy that you feel inside has brought into being the landscape around you.

Watch the clouds or the wind, changing from second to second. Feel the air on your skin. Feel the air entering and leaving your body, filling your lungs and sustaining your life from moment to moment.

Reflect how dependent you are on the landscape around you, on the extent to which your body has evolved to survive on the earth's surface. Try to still your mind and sit in silence, simply experiencing yourself as part of the landscape rather than as a detached observer.

Walking reflection: transience

Take half an hour to go for a walk. It can be in a city or in nature, but try at least to pass through some natural area, such as a park. Walk slowly, and as you walk, look at everything around you. Let your attention rest on whatever comes before your eyes.

As you do so, repeat the phrase 'Arising, passing away' in your mind. Whatever you see, contemplate whether it is now arising, like a flower in bud, or passing away, like a rotting tree trunk.

Once you have looked at a thing, look closer, within the flower; or look closely at the bark of the tree trunk. All the while, keep the phrase going in your mind, 'Arising, passing away'.

When you have looked closely, widen your vision again; not just the flower, but the whole plant; not just the tree trunk, but the whole forest.

As you go, you can touch, feel, smell and listen, as well as look – the feel of a patch of moss, the sound of a flute. Arising, passing away.

As you go, you can pause to reflect:

- Can I find a single thing that doesn't arise or pass away?
- How do I feel when you see something arising? How do I feel when you see something passing away?
- Why do things arise? Why do things pass away?
- Where do things go when they pass away? Where do things come from as they arise?

Find somewhere to sit down. Be aware of your body, feel its solidity, its warmth. Be aware of the blood running through your veins, and the rise and fall of your breath. As you give your attention to your body, keep the phrase turning, 'Arising, passing away'. After a few more minutes, let go of the phrase and relax.

8

Dance, Dance, Dance

IN THE PRECEDING CHAPTERS, I've suggested a few of the ways in which we might tread the Bodhisattva path in today's world. Through generosity and sharing, we build community and trust in the midst of a fragmented world. In connecting with others, we draw upon strengths and resources not available to us individually. In making practical ethical changes and simplifying our everyday lives, we come back into a loving relationship with nature and other people. In acting in many different ways to bring about change, we draw upon ever deeper reserves of energy and patience. Through meditation, we can offer the gift of stillness and centredeness to a distracted world. And in opening to the beauty of nature, reflecting on the Buddha's teachings, we can learn to see the world afresh in a way that opens our hearts to compassion.

While this is described as a path, it's not that each of these is a separate step along the way. The path is our life, and the practices and qualities of the Bodhisattva are what might unfold in us as we make our journey. While there may be times when we need to focus more on one than another, we need never to lose sight of any of them.

Total ecology

This is what distinguishes the path of Buddhism as environmentalism. It is not based exclusively on lifestyle changes, nor on technology, nor on activism, nor on a love of nature. It is not a political position, nor an academic theory. It does not attribute the environmental crisis to any single cause. Instead, what is called for by the suffering of the world is a total response. It involves how we look after our bodies, the technologies we use, how we relate to others one to one, how we come together collectively in our political and economic institutions, the cultures we create and pass on to future generations, the inner workings of our hearts and minds, and our most deeply held assumptions about who we are and our place in the world.

What is more, each of these areas of our lives is intimately interwoven with each of the others. If I earn my living working in a co-operative, I am inspiring others to find new ways of working together; if I protest peacefully, I am breaking the cycles of conflict; if I buy organic vegetables, I am cleaning the land; if I let go of the anxiety in my mind, I free up energy to work for others. In this view, ecology is not just the web of interconnections in the ecosystems that we call the natural world. We are included too – our minds, hearts, voices as well as our bodies. It includes our cultures, governments, corporations, communities and our most deeply held assumptions.

Je Tsongkhapa, one of the early figures of Tibetan Buddhism, who inspired a great ethical and social renewal in his own time, stresses the implications for this in everything we do:

So sensitive an ecology is the interdependence of all, that the slightest attention and assistance to others creates moral elevation for ourselves and humanity, while the slightest indifference or neglect towards others creates moral harm for ourselves and our civilization.[74]

To really understand this truth is to come fully alive. Not only does it impress on us the need to take responsibility for our thoughts, words, and actions, but it also imbues each one of them with a vibrant significance.

Emergence

An implication of this is that we never know what might result from what we do or say, even in the apparently mundane, ordinary times of our lives. The Buddha taught that wholesome actions, based on love and clarity, will bring happiness; and that unwholesome actions, based on selfishness and ignorance, will bring unhappiness. But as to how exactly those consequences unfold, we can never tell. Sometimes, some consequences are fairly predictable, but our actions can also extend way beyond what we can see or even imagine.

There is, in ecological thinking, a phenomenon known as emergence. It can, in fact, be found at all levels of reality, from sub-atomic particles to cellular biology to global ecology. Large-scale effects or patterns emerge, in quite unexpected ways, from the sum total of smaller scale patterns or behaviours.

I became interested in this some years ago when I was observing the behaviour of ants. I was on a long retreat in Spain, and would sometimes pass the long hot afternoons by making small piles of toenails and bits of dead skin on a rock. I noticed that sooner or later an ant would happen along and take a piece of detritus on its back and walk away. And once one ant had found the pile, others would appear as if by magic and, before long, the whole pile would be efficiently transported away.

At the time, I was mystified how the other ants were all alerted so quickly. I later learnt that ants do this not by directly communicating a message 'there is a pile of toenails on that rock.' Rather, each ant leaves behind a trail of pheromones. All each ant has to do is to follow a very simple rule and follow the pheromone trail back to the source of food. On their own, these very simple behaviours have little effect. If you put one ant in a room with a food source, it will wander at random until it finds it, which could be a very long time. But if you put a hundred ants in a room, those individual simple rules combine into a very efficient foraging machine. Together, the ants are complex and efficient in a way that none of them could be on their own.

The same goes for ant colonies, which are highly specialized structures, not unlike cities. They have the equivalents of dormitory suburbs, cemeteries, waste dumps, motorways, nurseries, and supermarkets, all appropriately placed in relation to each other. But ants don't have organizers or town planning departments. These patterns just emerge from the sum total of many ants following very simple rules.

The lesson I draw from this is not that we should all behave so mechanistically as ants, but rather that you don't always know the consequences of your actions. You may connect with someone by, say, having a passing conversation, and think no more of it. But you never know how, in the bigger picture of trillions of connections and conversations, what great changes might emerge from the small things you say or do.

I think the pattern of emergence can apply within our own lives, too. When you live your whole life from positive values, with a sense of purpose that includes your own needs but also looks beyond them, then something creative and unexpected happens. Your life takes on a sort of unity and become greater than the sum of its parts. Just as, in nature, from the ecology of a number of plants and animals, there might emerge some higher order, an ecosystem; or from a collection of cells, there might emerge a flower, so, out all that we do in the minutes, hours, and days of our lives, an overarching story emerges.

The nature of change

There are two ways of thinking about how we bring about change, whether we are talking about changing ourselves or changing the world. The first is to make a plan and execute it. I want lunch, so I go and make a sandwich; there is some environmental law that I want to support, so I email my elected representative. The second view of change is to wait and see what turns up, to be open to whatever changes might emerge in your life or in the world. I want a new job, so I see if anyone makes me any offers; my local beach is dirty, so I trust that something will be done about it.

In practice, we need both of these. If we have only the first, we can get things done but our lives are dry and uninspired, and we lose sight of the bigger picture. If we have only the second, our inspiration is wasted because we're so impractical we can't put anything into effect. So we need a combination of them, or a kind of dance between them. We need to both act in a grounded way, while also being open to things unfolding in ways we would never have imagined. You try meditation to see what it might be like; you start an environmental group and see who turns up. This is life lived more like an unfolding journey or adventure. Who knows where it might lead?

Dance, Dance, Dance

This perspective is especially needed at the current time. Global change comes slowly – there is a long lag between changes we make individually and their wider effects. If we just have a mechanistic view of change, we will be easily discouraged. If we just trust in wider change without actually doing anything, it will never come about. In being both grounded enough to keep on going, and open enough to see the wider possibilities, that we make change possible.

It is also when we are alive to both the first and second ways in which change happens that something greater emerges. It is right in the heart of our ordinary day-to-day activity, fraught as it may be with all sorts of anxiety and uncertainty, that there emerges the greater story of the meaning of our life and our place in the world. In beginning to discover this, we are not only tapping into a power to bring about change, but are also finding our way to our own deepest happiness. Personal happiness, viewed in this way, is not a luxury but a responsibility. The future of life, indeed, may even depend on us finding a way of living happily, and even blissfully, with each other and with the Earth.

To be alive to our story is to enter a more mythical, though no less real, realm. Being conscious of it is to see the mythic in the midst of the ordinary and awakens new strengths and qualities. An old Tibetan text, the *Kalachakra Tantra*, foretells of a time when the world will be in great danger from destructive forces. According to this text, just at the time when things are looking bleakest, there will arise into the world the realm of Shambhala. The warriors of Shambhala will arise in many different lands. They won't be joined in one organization; and they won't be recognizable by any uniform. But they will meet the forces that threaten life and usher in a new realm in which people live in harmony with each other and with nature, in which 'grain shall grow in the wild and the trees shall bow with fruit'.[75]

In some words attributed to Robert Thurman:

Shambhala is the critical mass of people making that shift in their hearts from despair, paranoia, fear, and egotism to openness, vulnerability, and optimism. And we can be in Shambhala now, rather than wanting it to arrive sometime later. If there is going to be a point, some critical moment when lots of people turn round at once and there's a massive awakening, that's good, but it will only happen because each individual person awakens in her or his own heart. One by one, the world will awaken.[76]

The weapons that the warriors wield are not swords and spears, but rather wisdom and compassion. Both individually and collectively, what keeps us from Shambhala is not some external army, but our own deluded clinging and the divisions we place between us. To free ourselves from their power, we need what has been called a 'new and wiser innocence, that combines the wonder of a child with the wisdom of a sage'.[77] We need to act more and more from a sense of purpose that transcends our own egos. We need hearts that don't shrink from the sight of suffering, and are not overwhelmed by it. We need to be alive, even in the thick of action, to the profound significance of each moment. At our disposal, we need to have the unified energy of trained minds; and a new language, that speaks from the heart. And there are other qualities that we need to build a more peaceful, sustainable world. The world does not need yet another army with serried ranks, but a living culture, sangha, or fellowship in which our hidden strengths will come to life. We will need Shambhala healers, poets, wizards, mothers, lovers, artisans, and many more. In our ordinary everyday lives, in the shadow of danger, we can each unfold our own story. To paraphrase Primo Levi, if not us, who? And if not now, when?[78]

Epilogue:
The Shambhala
Warrior Mind Training

Firmly establish your intention to live your life for the healing of the world. Be conscious of it, honour it, nurture it every day.

Be fully present in our time. Find the courage to breathe in the suffering of the world. Allow peace and healing to breathe out through you in return.

Do not meet power on its own terms. See through to its real nature – mind and heart made. Lead your response from that level.

Simplify. Clear away the dead wood in your life. Look for the heartwood and give it the first call on your time, the best of your energy.

Put down the leaden burden of saving the world alone. Join with others of like mind. Align yourself with the forces of resolution.

The Shambala Warrior Mind Training

Hold in a single vision, in the same thought, the transformation of yourself and the transformation of the world. Live your life around that edge, always keeping it in sight.

As a bird flies on two wings, balance outer activity with inner sustenance.

Following your heart, realize your gifts. Cultivate them with diligence to offer knowledge and skill to the world.
Train in non-violence of body, speech and mind. With great patience to yourself, learn to make beautiful each action, word and thought.

In the crucible of meditation, bring forth day by day into your own heart the treasury of compassion, wisdom and courage for which the world longs.

Sit with hatred until you feel the fear beneath it. Sit with fear until you feel the compassion beneath that.

Do not set your heart on particular results. Enjoy positive action for its own sake and rest confident that it will bear fruit.

When you see violence, greed and narrow-mindedness in the fullness of its power, walk straight into the heart of it, remaining open to the sky and in touch with the earth.

Staying open, staying grounded, remember that you are the inheritor of the strengths of thousands of generations of life.

Staying open, staying grounded, recall that the thankful prayers of future generations are silently with you.

Saving the Earth

Staying open, staying grounded, be confident in the magic and power that arise when people come together in a great cause. Staying open, staying grounded, know that the deep forces of Nature will emerge to the aid of those who defend the Earth. Staying open, staying grounded, have faith that the higher forces of wisdom and compassion will manifest through our actions for the healing of the world.

When you see weapons of hate, disarm them with love.

When you see armies of greed, meet them in the spirit of sharing.

When you see fortresses of narrow-mindedness, breach them with truth.

When you find yourself enshrouded in dark clouds of dread, dispel them with fearlessness.

When forces of power seek to isolate us from each other, reach out with joy.

In it all and through it all, holding to your intention, let go into the music of life. Dance!

Recommended Reading

General Buddhism

Chris Pauling, *Introducing Buddhism*,
Windhorse Publications, Birmingham, 2004.

Tejananda, *The Buddhist Path to Awakening*,
Windhorse Publications, Birmingham, 1999.

Ethics

Marshall B. Rosenberg, *Nonviolent Communication: A
Language of Compassion*, Puddledancer, Encinitas, 1999.

Sangharakshita, *Living Ethically*, Windhorse Publications,
Cambridge, 2009.

Meditation

Paramananda, *Change Your Mind: A Practical Guide to
Buddhist Meditation*, Windhorse Publications,
Birmingham, 1996.

Buddhism, the Environment, and Politics

David Edwards, *The Compassionate Revolution: Radical
Politics and Buddhism*, Green Books, Totnes, 1998.

Joanna Macy, *World as Lover, World as Self*,
Parallax, Berkeley, 1991.

Saving the Earth

Melvin McLeod (ed.), *Mindful Politics: A Buddhist Guide to Making the World a Better Place*, Wisdom Publications, Boston, 2006.

David R. Loy, *The Great Awakening: A Buddhist Social Theory,* Wisdom Publications, Boston, 2005.

John Stanley and David R. Loy, *A Buddhist Response to the Climate Emergency*, Wisdom Publications, Boston, 2009.

Ken Jones, *New Social Face of Buddhism: A Call to Action*, Wisdom Publications, Boston, 2005.

Mary Evelyn Tucker and Duncan Ryuken Williams, *Buddhism and Ecology*, Harvard University Press, Cambridge, 1998.

Donald Rothberg, *The Engaged Spiritual Life: A Buddhist Approach to Transforming Ourselves and the World*, Beacon Press, Boston, 2007.

Reflections and Exercises

Wes Nisker, *Buddha's Nature: Who We Really Are and Why This Matters*, Rider, London, 1998.

Joanna Macy and Molly Young Brown, *Coming Back to Life: Practices to Reconnect Our Lives, Our World*, New Society, Canada, 1998.

Paramananda, *A Deeper Beauty: Buddhist Reflections on Everyday Life*, Windhorse Publications, Birmingham, 2001.

Recommended Reading

John Seed et al. *Thinking Like a Mountain: Towards a Council of All Beings*, New Society, Canada, 1988.

Chris Johnstone, *Find Your Power: Boost Your Inner Strengths, Break Through Blocks and Achieve Inspired Action*, Nicholas Brealey Publishing, London, 2006.

Fiction

Jean Giono, *The Man Who Planted Trees*, London, Harvill, 1995.

Useful Websites

www.buddhafield.com (outdoor and ecological Buddhist retreats and festivals)

www.ecobuddhism.org (an international Buddhist campaign with an emphasis on climate change)

www.ecodharma.com (articles on ecological Buddhism and a centre in the Catalan Pyrenees)

www.ecopractice.fwbo.org (environmental resources within the Friends of the Western Buddhist Order)

www.greatturningtimes.org (Great Turning Times newsletter)

www.joannamacy.net (articles, resources and contacts for The Work that Reconnects)

www.350.org (campaigning for the 350ppm carbon dioxide target)

Notes and References

1. Peter Bennetts & Tony Wheeler, *Time & Tide: The Islands of Tuvalu*, Lonely Planet, Hawthorn, 2001.

2. http://www.wateraid.org/uk/what_we_do/the_need/disease/684.asp

3. *Climate Change 2007: Synthesis Report, An Assessment of the Intergovernmental Panel on Climate Change, Summary for Policymakers*, p.5. Intergovernmental Panel on Climate Change. http://www.ipcc.ch/pdf/assessment-report/ar4/syr/ar4_syr_spm.pdf

4. Waste Watch, www.wasteonline.org.uk

5. J.H. Lawton, *Extinction Rates*, Oxford University Press, 1995.

6. (ref to "a hundred and a thousand times greater than it was before humans appeared. It also seems to be increasing") cited at http://www.msnbc.msn.com/id/6502368/

7. Edward O.Wilson, *The Future of Life*, Abacus, London, 2003, cited at http://www.aei.org/article/14940

8. Sriyanie Miththapala, *Conserving Medicinal Species*, Ecosystems and Livelihoods Group, International Union for Conservation of Nature and Natural Resources, 2006, p.57.

9. WWF International, Institute of Zoology and Global Footprint Network, Living Planet Report 2008, p.2. Available at http://assets.panda.org/downloads/living_planet_report_2008.pdf

10. Colin D. Butler, '*Globalisation, Population, Ecology and Conflict*', *Health Promotion Journal of Australia*, 18(2), 2007, pp. 89-91.

11. Prof. Colin Butler, '*No Time to Nitpick about Climate*', *A Letter to the Medical Observer*, Australia, 15 August 2008.

12. Karl Marx, '*Theses on Feuerbach*', 1845, cited in G.N.Kitching, *Karl Marx and the Philosophy of Praxis*, Routledge, London, 1988, p.29.

13. For a much fuller exploration of the evolution of self awareness, see Robin Cooper, *The Evolving Mind: Buddhism, Biology, and Consciousness*, Windhorse Publications, Birmingham, 1996.

14. See Christopher S. Queen & Sallie B. King (eds), *Engaged Buddhism: Buddhist Liberation Movements in India*, State University of New York Press, Albany, 1996, p. 17ff.

15. Tom Athanasiou and Paul Beer, *Where We Stand: Honesty about Dangerous Climate Change, and about Preventing it*, Silver City, NM

Notes and References

and Washington DC, Foreign Policy in Focus, December 7 2005: http://www.fpif.org/fpiftxt/2973.

16. An unnamed former director of Greenpeace, quoted in Tom Athanasiou, *Slow Reckoning: The Ecology of a Divided Planet*, Secker & Warburg, London, 1997.

17. For more details on the 'six perfections', see Sangharakshita, *A Survey of Buddhism*, Windhorse Publications, Birmingham, 2001, p. 466ff.

18. Cited in Judith Herman, *Trauma and Recovery: The Aftermath of Violence from Domestic Abuse to Political Terror*, Basic Books, New York, 1997.

19. Culagosinga Sutta, Majjhima-Nikaya p.31

20. Helena Norberg-Hodge, *Ancient Futures: Learning from Ladakh*, Rider, London, 1992, p.137.

21. Thich Nhat Hanh, *Being Peace*, Parallax, Berkeley, 1987, pp. 11–12.

22. There is a growing trend seeking to replace the Gross National Product, which only measures financial transactions, with a measure that takes account of social, cultural, and environmental factors. The Government of Bhutan, for example, has introduced a measure of Gross National Happiness. See Jigmi Thinley, '*Gross National Happiness*', in *Mindful Politics: A Buddhist Guide to Making the World a Better Place*, Melvin McLeod (ed.), Wisdom Publications, Boston, 2006.

23. See http://www.idealist.org for a wide range of international volunteering opportunities.

24. See http://www2.btcv.org.uk and www.greenvolunteers.com.

25. See http://www.letslinkuk.org.

26. André Gorz, *Capitalism, Socialism, Ecology*, trans. Chris Turner, London: Verso, 1994, p. 4.

27. Tor Nørretranders, *The User Illusion: Cutting Consciousness Down To Size*, Penguin, London, 1999, p.406.

28. See Joanna Macy & Molly Young Brown, *Coming Back to Life: Practices to Reconnect Our Lives, Our World*, New Society Publishers, Gabriola Island, 1998.

29. Sangharakshita, *What is the Sangha?*, Windhorse Publications, Birmingham, 2001, pp. 241-242.

30. Kutadanta Sutta, *Digha-Nikaya* 5.22 ff.

31. P.D. Ryan, *Buddhism and the Natural World*, Windhorse Publications, Birmingham, 1998, p. 42.

32. See also chapter 1 of Joanna Macy, *World As Lover, World As Self*, Parallax Press, Berkeley, 1991.

33. H.H. the Dalai Lama, '*A New Approach to Global Problems*', in Melvin McLeod (ed.) *Mindful Politics, A Buddhist Guide to Making the World a Better Place*, Wisdom Publications, Boston, 2006, p.18ff.

34. Henry David Thoreau, *Walden, or Life in the Woods*, Forgotten Books, Mineola NY, 2008, p.63.

35. Details of the exercise, 'the Double Circle' in *Coming Back to Life*, p.146.

36. Sangharakshita, *Crossing the Stream*, Windhorse Publications, Birmingham, 1987, p.59.

37. 'Standby Britain: How it fuels our energy crisis', *The Independent*, 23 June 2005.

38. Energy Savings Trust, Press Release, 19 September 2003.

39. http://www.chooseclimate.org.

40. http://www.bbc.co.uk/radio4/youandyours/technology_launch.shtml

41. For a comprehensive overview of the effects of meat and dairy production, see *Food and Agriculture Organization of the United Nations, Livestock's Long Shadow: Environmental Issues and Options*, FAO, Rome, 2006, especially pp. 268-84. Available at http://www.fao.org/docrep/010/a0701e/a0701e00.htm

42. Bodhipaksa, *Vegetarianism* (revised edition), Windhorse Publications, Cambridge, 2009, p.52.

43. Gidon Eshel and Pamela Martin, '*Diet, Energy and Global Warming*', *Earth Interactions*, 2006 Vol. 10, p.18.

44. William Morris, *Hopes and Fears for Art*, Bibliolife, Charleston, SC, 2008, p.79.

45. Cited in David Yount, *How the Quakers Invented America*, Rowman and Littlefield, 2007, p.129.

46. Fore more advice on finding your way forward into constructive action, see *Find Your Power* by Chris Johnstone (see Further Reading, 'Reflections and Exercises')

47. http://www.transitiontowns.org.

48. J. Hansen *et al*, 'Target atmospheric CO_2: Where should humanity aim?' *Open Atmosphere Science Journal*, vol. 2, 2008, pp. 217-31.

49. Andrew Samuels, *The Political Psyche*, Routledge, London, 1993, p. 62.

50. Samvels, *op.cit.*, p. 103.

51. For a non-corporate perspective, see www.medialens.org.

52. Sangharakshita, *Know Your Mind: The Psychological Dimension of Ethics*

in Buddhism, Windhorse Publications, Birmingham, 1998, pp.164-8.

53. *The Dhammapada*, verse 5 as rendered by Ajahn Munindo, River Publications, Belsay, 2000.

54. This widely attributed quotation is probably apocryphal, but was at least in the spirit of her reply to the impudent young man. 'I did not believe that a Cause which stood for a beautiful ideal, for anarchism, should demand the denial of life and joy. I insisted that our Cause should not expect me to become a nun and that the movement should not be turned into a cloister. If it meant that, I did not want it. I want freedom, the right to self-expression, everybody's right to be beautiful, radiant things.' Emma Goldman, *Living My Life*, Dover Publications, Mineola NY, 1970, p.56.

55. http://www.climatecamp.org.uk.

56. The code of protest is no longer on the NEF website (www.newecon-omics.org) but is cited at http://www.iccwbo.org/iccbihi/index.html.

57. Marshall B. Rosenberg, *Nonviolent Communication: A Language of Life*, Puddle Dancer Press, Encinitas, CA, 2003, & the Center for Nonviolent Communication at http://www.cnvc.org.

58. Sangharakshita, *op.cit.*, pp.239 ff.

59. Paul H. Crompton (trans.) *Selections from the Embossed Tea Kettle*, Paul Crompton Ltd, London, 1986, p.45.

60. *The Dhammapada*, verses 1 & 2 as rendered by Ajahn Munindo, River Publications, Belsay, 2000.

61. This list is drawn from the *Satipatthana Sutta*. For a much fuller explo-ration, see the *Satipatthana Sutta* & commentaries: Sangharakshita, *Living with Awareness: A Guide to the Satipatthana Sutta*, Windhorse Publications, Birmingham, 2003 & Analayo, *Satipatthana: The Direct Path to Realization*, Windhorse Publications, Birmingham, 2006.

62. The chapter title is an often cited paraphrase from Fyodor Dostoevsky, *The Idiot*, Barnes & Noble, New York, 2004, p.351.

63. Quoted in Peter Marshall, *Nature's Web: Rethinking Our Place on Earth*, Cassell, London, 1992, p.349.

64. John Burroughs, '*The Art of Seeing Things*', in Allen Carlson and Sheila Linton (eds.) *Nature, Aesthetics and Environmentalism*, Columbia University Press, New York, 2008, p.80.

65. Arnold Berleant, quoted in Allen Carlson, '*Aesthetic Appreciation of the Natural Environment*', in Allen Carlson and Sheila Linton (eds.), *op. cit.*, pp. 124-5.

66. 'Naga Sutta: The Bull Elephant' (Ud 4.5), translated from the Pali by John D. Ireland. Access to Insight, June 7, 2009: http://www.access-toinsight.org/tipitaka/kn/ud/ud.4.05.irel.html.
67. 'Mahasaccaka Sutta, Majjhima-Nikaya' 31ff, in Bikkhu Nanamoli (trans.), *The Middle Length Discourses of the Buddha: A Translation of the Majjhima Nikaya*, Wisdom Publications, 1995, p.340.
68. Mahanidana Sutta, *Digha-Nikaya* p. 35.
69. Ki Tsurayuki, *Kokinshu (Collection of Poems Ancient and Modern)*, (c.905), cited by Geoffrey Bownas (trans.), Penguin Book of Japanese Verse, Penguin, London, 1998, p.lxii.
70. Nancy G. Hume (ed.), *Japanese Aesthetics and Culture: A Reader*, State University of New York Press, Albany, 1995, p.254.
71. Yoshida Kenko, *Essays in Idleness* (trans. G.B. Sansom), Wordsworth Editions, Ware, 1998, p.5.
72. Sangharakshita, *Wisdom Beyond Words*, Windhorse Publications, Birmingham, 2000, p.61.
73. Dilgo Khyentse Rinpoche: 'When you recognise the empty nature, the energy to bring about the good of others dawns, uncontrived and effortless', quoted in Melvin McLeod, *The Best Buddhist Writing 2005*, Shambhala, Boston, 2005, p.302.
74. Je Tsongkhapa, 'Twenty-Seven Verses on Mind Training', v.20., in Lex Hixon, *Mother of the Buddhas*, Quest Books, Wheaton, 1993, p.243.
75. For a fuller version of this myth, see www.joannamacy.net or Joanna Macy, *World as Lover, World as Self*, Parallax Press, Berkeley, 1991, chapter 16.
76. Attributed to Robert Thurman. The source cannot be traced, though in correspondence he said 'If I didn't say it, I should have, and I probably did... It's not a matter of waiting for some external cataclysm and external salvation afterwards; it's a matter of turning round within oneself, seeing the world of conflicting egotisms as a kind of ongoing cataclysm and opting out of it.'
77. Primo Levi, *If Not Now, When?*, Abacus, London, 1984.
78. http://www.kalachakranet.org/kalachakra_tantra_shambhala.html.

About Windhorse Publications

Windhorse Publications is a Buddhist publishing house, staffed by practising Buddhists. We place great emphasis on producing books of high quality, accessible and relevant to those interested in Buddhism at whatever level. Drawing on the whole range of the Buddhist tradition, our books include translations of traditional texts, commentaries, books that make links with Western culture and ways of life, biographies of Buddhists, and works on meditation.

As a charitable institution we welcome donations to help us continue our work. We also welcome manuscripts on aspects of Buddhism or meditation. To join our email list, place an order or request a catalogue please visit our website at www.windhorsepublications.com or contact:

Windhorse Publications
38 Newmarket Road
Cambridge CB5 8DT
UK

Perseus Distribution
1094 Flex Drive
Jackson TN 38301
USA

Windhorse Books
PO Box 574
Newtown NSW 2042
Australia

About the FWBO

Windhorse Publications is an arm of the Friends of the Western Buddhist Order, which has more than sixty centres on five continents. Through these centres, members of the Western Buddhist Order offer regular programmes of events for the general public and for more experienced students. These include meditation classes, public talks, study on Buddhist themes and texts, and bodywork classes such as t'ai chi, yoga, and massage. The FWBO also runs several retreat centres and the Karuna Trust, a fundraising charity that supports social welfare projects in the slums and villages of Southern Asia.

Many FWBO centres have residential spiritual communities and ethical businesses associated with them. Arts activities are encouraged too, as is the development of strong bonds of friendship between people who share the same ideals. In this way the FWBO is developing a unique approach to Buddhism, not simply as a set of techniques, but as a creatively directed way of life for people living in the modern world.

If you would like more information about the FWBO please visit the website at www.fwbo.org or write to:

London Buddhist Centre
51 Roman Road
London E2 0HU
UK

Arvaloka
14 Heartwood Circle
Newmarket NH 03857
USA

Sydney Buddhist Centre
24 Enmore Road
Sydney NSW 2042
Australia

Why not try A Buddhist View of…?

Meaning in Life

by Sarvananda

How can we bring more sense of significance into our lives?
What meaning does life have in the face of suffering or death?
Do we have a 'why' to live for?

Sarvananda draws a parallel between the Buddha's quest and
our own search for meaning in the modern world. Using
references from the 20th century, he covers many of the ways
in which we seek meaning, citing writers and thinkers such as
Akira Kurosawa, Wordsworth and Woody Allen. In so doing
he moves from individual understanding to the principles of
Buddhist teaching and demonstrates in a calm, friendly way
how to apply the teachings practically, before finally taking
the reader to a deeper reality.

A concise, witty exploration of what truly matters.

ISBN 9781 899579 87 7
£7.99 / $13.95 / €9.95
128 pages

Why not try A Buddhist View of…?

Vegetarianism

by Bodhipaksa

How does what we eat affect us and our world? Is there a connection between vegetarianism and living a spiritual life? Doesn't HH the Dalai Lama eat meat?

A trained vet, respected teacher and happy vegan, Bodhipaksa answers all of these questions and more. Tackling issues such as genetically modified vegetables and modern ways of producing food he dispels widespread myths and reflects upon the diets dominant in the contemporary West. In comparison, he considers the diets of wandering monks in Ancient India and the diet of the Buddha himself.

By considering why people eat meat and relating this to Buddhist ethics he explores habits and the possibility of change. He takes a positive view of the benefits of vegetarianism, and shows practically, how to maintain a healthy and balanced vegan or vegetarian lifestyle.

This exploration shows how a meat-free life can not only lighten the body but also the soul.

ISBN 9781 899579 96 9
£7.99 / $13.95 / €9.95
104 pages

Wildmind: A Step-by-Step Guide to Meditation

by Bodhipaksa

From how to build your own meditation stool to how a raisin can help you meditate, this illustrated guide explains everything you need to know to start or strengthen your meditation practice. This best-seller is in a new handy format and features brand new illustrations.

"Of great help to people interested in meditation and an inspiring reminder to those on the path."
-Joseph Goldstein, cofounder of the Insight Meditation Society and author of *One Dharma: The Emerging Western Buddhism*

"Bodhipaksa has written a beautiful and very accessible introduction to meditation. He guides us through all the basics of mindfulness and also loving-kindness meditations with the voice of a wise, kind, and patient friend."
-Dr. Lorne Ladner, author of *The Lost Art of Compassion*

ISBN 9781 899579 91 4
£11.99 / $18.95 / €15.95
264 pages